MW00323918

SAINT JOHN FISHER

St. John Fisher
Sketch by Peter Paul Rubens, after
Hans Holbein the Younger -British Museum

SAINT JOHN FISHER

by

FR. VINCENT MCNABB, O.P.

"Not that I condemn any other men's conscience.
"Their conscience may save them; and mine must save me."
(Words of Fisher to Cromwell)

Mediatrix Press
MMXV

ISBN: 0692446273

©Mediatrix Press, MMXV
http://www.mediatrixpress.com/

Originally Published by:
Sheed and Ward, 1936
This work is in the Public Domain

NIHIL OBSTAT:

        FR. ADRIANUS ENGLISH, O.P., S.T.L., B.Sc FR.
        RAYMUNDUS P. DEVAS, O.P.

IMPRIMATUR:

        FR. BERNARDUS DELANY, O.P., PRIOR
        PROVINCIALIS ANGLIAE
        IN FESTO STI. GEORGII, 1935.

NIHIL OBSTAT:

        THOMAS MCLAUGHLIN, S.Tn.D.
        CENSOR DEPUTATUS

S.TH. DATUR:

        ✠ JOSEPH BUTT
        VIC. CAP.
        WESTMONASTERII, DIE 16 APRILIS, 1935

Table of Contents

PETRO EPISCOPO SOUTHWARCIS S. JOANNIS
FISHER, MARTYRIS SUCCESSORI ET HEREDI IN
CURA PASTORALI ATQUE IN OBSEQUIO FILIALI
ERGA SUCCESSORES BEATI APOSTOLI PETRI

ST. JOHN FISHER

Introduction

 EAR reader! you are about to take part in perhaps the greatest tragedy of an age that wrote Hamlet and Macbeth. Greater even than the writer's part will be yours, the reader's and hearer's part. Only your hearing ear and your seeing eye will bring the tragedy to its own.

But your seeing eye and hearing ear must first recognise that a greater than Hamlet or Macbeth is here. They are but splendid fiction. But the tragedy of the first and only Cardinal to receive the martyr's crown is as real as the Yorkshire moors where John Fisher was born, or as Tower Hill where the Cardinal Bishop of Rochester was beheaded.

Do not expect anything melodramatic or miraculous in this tragedy of tragedies: all on the hero's side is as sober in colouring as the heather on a Yorkshire moor. All is as normal as the steadiness of the hills or the falling of flakes of snow.

Search as you may in the plain tale of this Yorkshireman who was spokesman of England's faith and chivalry, you will find no gesture, no stir, no noise, but only a humble self-distrusting quest of the best. But, dear reader, in this outwardly emotionless love of God and men to see a tragedy beyond all telling or seeing will call from you the best of your mind and heart.

"Truly it was a more glorious sight to see St. Paul, who got his living by his own great labour in hunger, thirst, watchings, in cold going wool-clad and bearing about the Gospel and law of Christ both upon the land and on the sea, than to behold now the Archbishops and Bishops in their apparel be it never so rich.

"In that time were no chalices of gold but there were many golden priests. Now be many chalices of gold and almost no golden priests.

"Truly neither gold, precious stones nor glorious bodily garments be not the cause wherefore kings and princes of the world should dread God and His Church, for doubtless they have far more worldly riches than we have. But holy doctrine, good life and example of honest conversation be the occasion whereby good and holy men (also wicked and cruel people) are moved to love and fear Almighty God."

It is one of these "golden priests" who thus sets out the programme of his life a few weeks after the Chief Bishop of the Church had named him to the poorest see of England.

I - A Saint's Boyhood

John Fisher, son of Robert Fisher, wool merchant, and Agnes, his wife, was born at

Beverley, a town in the East Riding of Yorkshire. His family were of such average English station that the year of his birth is unknown. The first clue to his birth-year is the record of the first great tragedy in his life. We are told that his father died whilst " he was still of a tender age." His father's will may still be seen in the British Museum. As it is dated A.D. 1477, and John was then of tender age, some of his biographers have not unlikely given his birth-year as 1469. Others give the year 1459. The matter is of some, but not vital importance.

Beverley of the late 15th century was Yorkshire in little; and by the wool from its moorland flocks Yorkshire of the late 15th century was in daily touch with the life, or at least the trading life of the compact thing called Europe. As early as 1276 a Florentine firm made a contract with the Cistercian Abbey of Fountains for their wool-crop of the following four years.

In the time of Henry II, Spanish merchants exported pieces of scarlet from Beverley to the Continent and "Beverley Blue" and "Scarlet Cloth" were famous abroad as early as the 13th century.

It was, therefore, into no uncultured by-way of the world that the son of Robert and Agnes Fisher was born. The unwalled town of timber-framed houses on the eastern moorlands of Yorkshire was hardly less than a busy suburb of the centres of European life. Some of the foreign buyers in his father's shop might tell travellers' tales of the slaughter of Christians at the taking of Constantinople. A Spaniard might rouse the boy's dormant faith by stories of Spain's great battlings with the Moors. A Florentine wool merchant might point to a passing Beverley Blackfriar and remark: "One of those Blackfriars—a Fra Girolamo Savonarola is rousing all Florence and half of Italy. He has had the foolhardiness to challenge my bankers, the Medici. The common people run after him; because they think he is a holy man, and he prophesies dreadful happenings if Catholics—priests and lay-folk—do not mend their ways."

A few minutes' walk from his father's shop, with its barter and talk, took him out into the great quiet of the Yorkshire moors. Nothing more than a clue is given to the place these moors took in his boyish life. When in the Tower awaiting death he wrote a little book to his half-sister, Elisabeth, a Dominican nun at Dartford.

It opens with a lengthy and realistic description of the hardships gladly borne by the hunters " who most early in the morning break their sleep, and rise when others do take their rest and ease. And in his labour he may use no plain highways and soft grass; but he must tread upon the fallows, run over the hedges, and creep through the thick bushes and cry all the long day upon his dogs; and so continue without meat or drink until the very night drive him home."

There is a tradition that this delightful introduction to a book on Religious Perfection came of the blessed man's delight in hare-coursing on his beloved Yorkshire moors. The little book is subtly autobiographical. Not only does it open a door to the boyish lure of the chase, but it opens a latchet-gate into this "Hound of Heaven's" untiring quest for God.

Amongst all the influences of his early life we must surely be right in giving first place to his mother. No doubt his father was of such an honest God-fearing type that his influence over his youngest son John would have been deep and lasting. But death divided father and son before the influence of the mother would have naturally given place to the influence of the father. Yet the influence of the father was felt, and felt deeply, in his giving his children such a mother. Whether consciously or unconsciously, Robert Fisher had acted on the principle that "A man, in marrying, should choose, not a good wife, but a good mother of his children."

When Agnes Fisher buried the father of her four children before the rood in St. Mary's Church, she carried out his will that he, a merchant of Beverley, should find his long home in the great church which shrined the merchants' and craftsmen's guilds. Perhaps in obedience to his wishes and for the good of these four children she chose a second husband named White. No breach in the continuity of the home seems to have been made. The three sons and one daughter only added to the store of family affections.

II - Family Council

In the will of Robert Fisher there is a clause bequeathing "to each of my children of my own property the sum of £2 13s. 4d."

We are told that making use of this bequest, Agnes Fisher put her sons Robert and John to the school of the great Collegiate Church of St. John. If no mention is made of the third, eldest son, the silence may mean that he was of an age when he would be of use in the business now endangered by the loss of his father.

The subsequent history of John Fisher's literary career clears from the charge of exaggeration the words of his biographer: "This our John Fisher so far excelled the rest of his schoolfellows in his learning that it was evident to see even then whereto he tended, and what he was like to prove unto in time to come."

Underneath the biographer's slight account of the boy's going from Beverley to Cambridge ("distant from his native soil about eight days' journey southward") there may be rescued a charming epic of family life: "After, when he came to more mature and wise years, his mother and other frendes (kinsfolk) being still careful of his well-doing began to consider among themselves for what trade of life he was most fit." Few parts even of Europe offered greater opportunities for the trade of money-making than were offered by the Yorkshire of that day. John's two elder brothers seem to have taken these opportunities. But John was a different problem for the mother and her kinsfolk. "After they had perceived in him a great dexterity and aptness for learning; and had further noted him to be (as he was indeed) naturally endowed with a sober and deep wit, a perfect and steadfast memory and a will prompt and forward to learn, they thought among themselves no way so good as to continue him at study, and thereupon by general consent he was sent to the University of Cambridge."

This is a most charming glimpse into a normal English home of the old Catholic days. There is the picture of the careful loving mother who feels that the future of this gifted son is a trust she owes to her dead husband. The picture is completed by that outline of something like a family council summoned to deal with an unusual situation—a Fisher who shows a decided inclination and indeed aptitude, not for business but for books! This miniature parliament meets to deal with a matter of urgency and to decide a Vote of Supply. The result of this family council is that young master Fisher leaves Beverley for Cambridge which then flowered in learning and was thoroughly frequented and furnished with Doctors and Fellows coming from all parts of England as of ancient time had been accustomed.

III - Cambridge

We are not sure that Master Melton, head of Michael House, Cambridge, found in his new student anything that he would call genius. The Yorkshire lad would not have impressed Cambridge so quickly and so deeply as a London lad, by name Thomas More, his contemporary, impressed Oxford.

But life in the little thriving town of Beverley had already called forth from the future Cardinal and martyr an attitude which was the foundation of his unique tragedy—an attitude of duty and an attitude of poverty.

His sense of duty was but a mystical flowering of his reverential fear of God. When as a boy of eight or thereabouts death came into his home to take the father of the home, the boy, whom we know best as a man, was such as to see in this lesson of death the responsibility of life. The John Fisher that we know at close quarters only when he has grown from boyhood to manhood leaves us with the impression of a serious-minded, duty-loving boy. In saying this we are far from suggesting that he was unlovable. Indeed, boyhood and a zeal "to be about his father's business," often make an irresistible appeal to our love.

The young Cambridge undergraduate who began his University career as the outcome of a family council and no doubt financial co-operation could hardly fail to learn the first of the beatitudes —"Blessed are the poor in spirit for theirs is the kingdom of heaven." By his "will and promptness to learn" he was to be one of the countless examples that it is not by riches but by poverty that men commonly reach the kingdom of science.

It was in the year 1483 that the lad John Fisher, aged some fourteen years, and clad perhaps in "Beverley Blue" went southward to Cambridge.

The next twenty years of his life had Cambridge almost for their only centre.

Michael House, where these twenty years were spent, had for master a Yorkshireman, William Melton. Towards his old college and his old master, Fisher gave the tribute of "his perfect and steadfast memory." As a scholar and saint he would remember his old master's scholarship and holiness. His old college was faithfully remembered by a gift of a hundred pounds in gold on that April day, 1534, when with a joyous face he left his home at Rochester for his martyr's crown. These hundred pounds in gold to his beloved Michael House were his sole legacy to any institution.

The academic career that opened before the young Yorkshire undergraduate is now little more than a series of dates: 1487, Bachelor; 1491, Master of Arts and Fellow of Michael House; 1497, Master of Michael House; D.D. and Vice-Chancellor; 1504, Chancellor.

Behind the almost monotonous list of dates lies the mysterious preparation of a mind and soul for the altitude of heroism.

It would be going beyond the evidence to see in the saint's academic career the trace of genius. His own account of the low ebb of learning in the University prepares us to realize that he could spend twenty years in its atmosphere without having a scholar's knowledge of Greek or Hebrew. But we are in touch with the quality which made him successively Master of Michael House, then Vice-Chancellor, and lastly Chancellor, when we read that twelve years after his consecration as Bishop and in his forty-seventh year he begins the serious study of Greek; and a year after, the study of Hebrew!

IV - Vera Effigies

The pen-portrait of him left by his anonymous biographer has the quiet confidence of a *vera effigies*.

"In stature of body he was tall and comely, exceeding the common and middle sort of men; for he was to the quantity of six foot in height. And being therewith very slender and lean, was nevertheless upright and well framed, straight-backed, big-jointed and strongly sinewed.

"His hair by nature black . . . his eyes large and round, neither full black nor full grey, but of a mixed colour between both, his forehead smooth and large . . . somewhat wide-mouthed and big-jawed as one ordained to utter speech much wherein was, notwithstanding a certain comeliness.

"Vainly or without cause he would never speak. Neither was his ordinary talk of common worldly matters, but rather of the divinity and high power of God—of the joys of heaven and the paines of hell—of the glorious death of martyrs and straight life of Confessors. . . .

"In study he was very laborious and painful, in preaching assiduous, ever beating down heresy and vice, in prayer most fervent and devout, in fasting, abstinence and punishing of his bare body rigorous without measure."

For lack of incidents in the student life of Fisher at Cambridge, we confidently set before our reader this picture drawn by one who knew him later on as Bishop and indeed as Confessor and Martyr. But no true pictures of the martyr could contradict each other. What he once was he had always been and would always be. There were no dislocations in his life. Indeed it would be true to say that there were no great visible crises in his life. His fellow-martyr St. Thomas More has a page of immortal literature describing in a letter to his beloved daughter Meg:

"How many a night he lay awake wrestling with the flesh that dreaded a martyr's death. If such hours of anguish ever came to the "slender, lean, tall Yorkshireman, whose talk was mostly about God, no one was ever ushered into secrets of that anguish. If he wrestled for his soul he wrestled, like Jacob, alone with God."

It was not genius, therefore, that gave him the full confidence first of his masters and then of his fellow-teachers in royal Cambridge. Some of the Bishops who, in the hour of trial, fell when he stood, were his contemporaries in the University. But though their academic success equalled or surpassed his, they never equalled the hold he had over their fellow-teachers because they were almost a world apart from this "wide-mouthed, big jawed" northerner who "in fasting, abstinence and punishing his bare body was rigorous beyond measure."

V - The Lady Margaret

In 1495 his quiet academic life was dramatically changed, without his knowing it, by a detail of his duty as senior proctor of the University. Business of the University took him to the Court of Henry VII, then at Greenwich. Amongst other items he has noted in his official log-book is: "I dined with the Lady Mother of the King. I supped with the Chancellor."

This Lady was no other than Margaret Beaufort, only child of John Beaufort, first Duke of Somerset, who came from Edward the Third through John of Gaunt. By her first husband Edmund of Tudor, Earl of Richmond, and brother of Henry VI, she had one child who was to become king of an undivided England as Henry VII. In bringing about the marriage of her king-son to Elizabeth of York, daughter of Edward IV, she brought to an end the suicidal Wars of the Roses. Few women deserve so well of English history. From the gift of peace which has won her country's gratitude she was led, as we shall see, by this Cambridge proctor to win still further and more lasting gratitude by her gifts to learning.

A hardly less historical character was Fisher's host of the evening meal. "My Lord Chancellor" was no other than Cardinal Morton, the life-long friend and counsellor and protector of the Countess Margaret. In his skilful hands lay the destinies of the kingdom. To stand well with him was already to have begun success. One of his late household, Fisher's fellow-martyr, Thomas More, was even now following the law-studies which would make him a fellow-Chancellor of the great Cardinal.

For the moment we need only try to call up the "dinner with the Lady Mother of the King—supper with the Chancellor." Many of his contemporary fellow-teachers and all his subsequent fellow-Bishops would have looked on those two meals as the prelude or possibility of a successful worldly career.

All we know of our saint would have to be denied if we thought he looked on his supper with the Chancellor and dinner with the King's mother as anything but a temptation to pride or ambition. The arts of advancement in worldly success were unknown or could only be unprized by this scholar whose quest was along the path of duty and truth. Nor can this view be reckoned as mere conjecture when we remember that it was seven years before that dinner with the two greatest powers except the king, did bring any favours to the young priest.

We have said "young priest," lest we forget that this "senior proctor" of the University was but twenty-six years—not quite half the years of the Countess of Richmond who was then in her fifty-fourth year.

It was in 1502, when Fisher was thirty-three and the Countess was sixty-one, that he became her chaplain. For the next seven years the history of the Countess and her chaplain is a unique page of sanctity expressing itself as scholastic munificence.

Two things claim our notice in this fascinating page or English hagiography: first, the saint's relation to the royal widow; and secondly, the saint's zeal for learning.

Between the two souls, so far apart in age and social position, there was another bond than that of penitent and confessor. By every instinct of his soul he was "A flower of English knighthood" in an age when chivalry had been killed by the thing that was producing or welcoming such books as *Il Principe* of Machiavelli. His chivalrous relation with his royal penitent once became vocal and eloquent some nineteen years after the two had been parted by death. The book he wrote in defence of the Blessed Sacrament against Oecolampadius (1526) was dedicated to Bp. Richard Fox of Winchester. In this dedication the memory of his dead patroness and penitent moved him to unlock his heart with these poignant words: "There are perhaps many who believe that his (Henry VII's) mother, the Countess of Richmond and Derby, that noble and incomparable lady, dear to me by so many titles obtained the bishopric for me by her prayers to her son.

"But the facts are entirely different . . . I do not say this to diminish my debt of gratitude to that excellent lady. My debts are indeed great. Were there no other besides the great and sincere love which she bore to me above all others (as I know for a certainty); yet what favour could equal such a love on the part of such a princess?

"But besides her love she was most munificent towards me. For though she conferred on me no ecclesiastical benefice she had the desire if it could be done to enrich me . . . This only I will add, that though she chose me as her director to hear her confessions and to guide her life, yet I gladly confess that I learnt more from her great virtue then ever I could teach her."

Perhaps the most fundamental phrase in this jet of memory is "if it could be done." The truth is that even if an angel from heaven had tried to enrich the Bishop of England's poorest bishopric it could not be done.

A touching sign of the saint's unique relations with Margaret has found an unexpected place in the Statutes which he drew up for St. John's College, Cambridge, which he founded. He willed that as he was to be prayed for at Mass, so also should the Lady Margaret, "for he was indebted to her as to his own mother." From this almost sole reference to his mother we may perhaps gather that Agnes Fisher had been called by death from her second family whilst they were still too young to know their loss. The cultured courtly woman whose years were twice those of her confessor may have seen not only into a soul that sought God alone, but into a human heart that needed a little mothering to bring out its best.

VI - Learning in Ruins

We have said that the seven years of spiritual fellowship with the holy Countess of Richmond are largely filled with the history of their joint work for education. After her death that work was carried on by the survivor with the added zeal of a dedication.

It is not always realized how necessary was an educational revival such as became the purpose of the Countess and her confessor. Four years after Fisher became Lady Margaret's confessor (and almoner!) he welcomed as Chancellor, King Henry VII. In his official address he said: "Either from continual lawsuits and wrongs inflicted by the town or from long-continued pestilence, by which we lost many of our most cultured men, and no less than ten grave and very learned doctors, or from the want of any patrons and benefactors of arts and letters, studies began generally to languish so that . . . we should have fallen into utter desolation." The Chancellor, though a loyal subject of his king, was too loyal a subject of the truth to offer his king a gross exaggeration under the cover of a compliment.

One cause of the decay of learning may have escaped the thought of the Chancellor, or may not have been a dish fit to "set before a king." England had spent something like a century in civil war. During that period it was not book lore, but warlore, that counted. War at all times weakens the pulse of scholarship. But civil war weakens it to the point of death.

The son of a Yorkshire wool-mercer would have an opportunity of seeing the subjects and officials of the Church and indeed of the State become only something less than the carriers of a social disease. Their vast celibate organizations of lands and landworkers, provided the means of easy taxation for royal and papal wants. If these wants had always been civil and ecclesiastical needs the final hurt would not have been so disastrous. But these wants were so often for the purpose of war, and her celibate monks were, on the whole, such economical administrators that an abbey became little more than a royal estate with contemplative monks as rent-and-rate collectors.

If Meaux with its 11,000 sheep and 1,000 cattle in 1280 can be taken as typical of the development of the contemplative, we can see what effects war had on religion and learning.

The great Cistercian abbeys of Fisher's native county were amongst the richest in Europe. A recent study of them, though made sympathetically by a Catholic and a priest, provides us with facts which must have influenced the educational aims of Fisher. These great Cistercian abbeys that counted their lands by thousands of acres, and their stock by tens of thousands of cattle were a strange anticlimax to the romantic reform practically begun by St. Bernard. A certain, not unnatural, inclination for bigness had ended by subordinating the monk to the thing. In the end, with these contemplative monks, who embodied an idea necessary for the health of the life in England, book-lore, whether religious or profane, could hardly have been a staple monastic product.

VII - The Plight of Preaching

Light is thrown on Fisher's concern for education by a letter of Edward Lee, Archbishop of York, in 1535. The significance of the Archbishop's remark has not escaped the alert scholarship of G. Constant from whose masterly work *The English Schism* (p. 19) we will quote it: "In 1535, Edward Lee, Archbishop of York, bewailed the fact that he had not twelve secular priests capable of preaching; that with the exception of a few Dominicans none of the religious were trained to preach."

Undoubtedly England was the richest and best organized Church in the West. But the very perfection and elaborateness of its organization, which was once its strength, became its weakness. The passage from strength to weakness was so gradual that it was imperceptible and almost inevitable. The less than twelve secular priests of the vast diocese of York who were capable of preaching were no whit the more secure of their living than were the hundreds of their fellow-priests who could not preach.

Men, and even good men, living in such a system might be excused from realising that a parochial organization based on a state-guaranteed income can be apostolic only by a kind of miracle. Moreover, into such a highly organized system the apostolic work which might rightly be expected from mendicant and itinerant friars could come only as an interruption or an interference.

The intellectual lethargy which this system fostered was almost the beginning of a virtue. Jesus Our Saviour had assuredly not come into the world to encourage classical studies or develop the physical sciences. The Incarnation was not primarily towards Delphine editions or aeroplanes. What Jesus taught was apostolic truths which men should live. But when, by no fault chargeable to any individual, the apostolic life was psychologically impossible to the secular clergy and ecclesiastically impossible to the regular clergy the refusal to spend time on the classics or the physical sciences was not necessarily an intellectual, and still less a moral vice.

The joint educational activities of Fisher and Lady Margaret are in two groups and in each group are two undertakings. The first group comprises the Lady Margaret Chairs of Divinity at Oxford and Cambridge (1503) and a preacher-ship of six yearly sermons (1504). The second group comprised the foundation of Christ's College (1505) and St. John's (1516) in his own University of Cambridge.

The details of these educational efforts of the Countess and her confessor are no little part of the saint's tragic life. The Lady Margaret Chairs of Divinity were an attempt—and, as the sequel shows, a belated attempt—to give the thousands of parochial clergy of England a modest sufficiency of dogmatic theology. The duties of the foundation were a daily lecture during the greater part of the year except in Lent if the Chancellor thought Lenten sermons more useful."

Such an arrangement springing from the mind of the young Vice-Chancellor, then in his thirty-fourth year, was criticism only half-veiled by royal munificence. That Oxford accepted what it could easily call interference from Cambridge was clearly not due to the reputation of the young Vice-Chancellor but of his royal patroness.

The Statutes of St. Catherine's throw light on this bold move of the young Cambridge Vice-Chancellor to give Theology a position of honour at the two Universities. Robert Woodlark, Provost of the great Royal College of King's, had no doubt seen that University education was largely tending to provide, not men of God, but king's men. To arrest the tendency he did two unique things. He was the only Head of one college who founded another college. Moreover, by the Statutes which he gave to his college which he founded in 1475, he laid it down that the study of Canon Law and Civil Law was to be excluded. Woodlark, though a scholar fit to be a Provost of King's College, was cleric enough to know that a University which is providing Tudor monarchs with keen lawyers and administrators is not about the King of Kings' business. The history of the "Hierarchy which failed" justified the fine intuitions of the Provost Woodlark. Cambridge of the late 15th century was too small a town, and

Provost Woodlark's action too unprecedented that it could be unknown to the Vice-Chancellor who a few years later founded a Chair for providing sound theological lectures for future priests.

VIII - "If Leave be given"

With Fisher's statute allowing the Lady Margaret Professors to substitute sermons for lectures during Lent we pass from the first to the second of his undertakings—the endowment of a special preacher. The terms of this preaching endowment complete a minor part in the quiet tragedy of Fisher's martyred life. "The preacher was to preach six sermons and receive £10 a year. Once every two years on a Sunday he was to preach at St. Paul's; but if leave was not given, at St. Margaret's, Westminster; but again if leave was again refused, at some church in London! Once every two years in some feast day in each of the churches of WARE and CHESHUNT in Hertfordshire; BASSINGBOURNE, ORWELL and BABRAHAM in Cambridgeshire; and MAXEY, ST. JAMES DEEPING, ST. JOHN DEEPING, BOURN BOSTON and SWINESHEAD in Lincolnshire."

The proviso if leave was not given strikes a tragic note. Something of the same apostolic boldness that had provided a special lecturer in Divinity for Oxford was attempting to provide, every two years, a special preacher for London—the London on which Galt has fastened the epithet—"that dormitory of cumbrous divines." But Fisher was already aware of the difficulties arising from vested ecclesiastical interests and very efficient but complicated ecclesiastical machinery. Lady Margaret might guarantee the stipend for the sermon. But no one could guarantee if the vested interests would allow the sermon to be preached. Yet *Verbum Dei non est alligatum.*

The eleven other towns (as Boston) or villages (as Ware and Cheshunt) were in the provinces. But preaching was such a lost art that even a good sermon once every two years was worth the trouble of organising and endowing.

Not insignificant is Fisher's condition that this preacher "should be unbeneficed but should be a perpetual fellow of some college in Cambridge." This condition bears pathetic witness to Fisher's unique zeal to wed even the New Learning as it was called with the Old Faith, lest the word of a French rationalist should be realized and the "Printing Press should destroy the Church."

Not everyone who studies the change of religion in England has seen how great a part was played by the traffic centres of the kingdom. London and East Anglia, the most important of these centres, were justifying the wise advice of Aquinas that a country should depend as much as possible on home-growth and as little as possible on foreign trade, lest foreign influences backed by money power should corrupt home institutions. Fisher's mind was so sensitive to the intellectual and religious currents of his time that his founding a preachership for London and East Anglia may have been a scholar's and a saint's reading the signs of the times.

IX - A Patroness of Learning

The Lady Margaret Professorship and Preachership were Fisher's hurried action to stem disaster. But it was followed by the necessarily more deliberate action of founding two Cambridge Colleges, viz., Christ's College and St. John's.

The founding of Christ's College for a Master, 12 Fellows and 47 Scholars (in all 60) was made easy by the affection which Henry VII had for his mother, the Lady Margaret. On the other hand the founding of St. John's was made almost impossible because the affection which Henry VII had for his mother did not pass from father to son. Though the Lady Margaret had bequeathed a considerable sum for the founding of St. John's, Henry VIII began his adventure in Tudor Totalitarianism by confiscating his grandmother's bequest. This earnest of Bluff King Hal's educational policy would have killed St. John's in the womb had not the group of Lady Margaret's executors included the young Yorkshireman, now Bishop of Rochester. No other of the executors dared to withstand the young king, whose royal revels were even then being financed by a conversion of royal capital into royal income.

Fisher's boldness did not stop the royal thief. Yet we are glad that what the grandson stole from his saintly and munificent grandmother was made good by the poorest of England's bishops in gratitude to Lady Margaret and to learning.

X - The Saint's Library

Fisher's patronage of learning, indeed of the New Learning, was not the prevalent patronage given by the nouveaux riches; it was a scholar's love of scholarship raised from a passion to a devotion by a saint's love of God. The tragedy of a book-lover who was an open-handed scholar is in every word of the old manuscript life in its account of his founding of St. John's:

"Thus did this godly man not only bestow his labour, care and study in executing the will of the noble Lady (Margaret) the foundress, but . . . his library of books (which was thought to be such as no Bishop in Europe had the like) . . . he gave long before his death to the College of St. John by a deed of gift, and put his house in possession thereof by gift of his own hand. And then by Indenture borrowed all the said books to have the use thereof for life."

Of this library with its unique collection of books, his friend Erasmus wrote, alarmed about the Bishop's health: "Your library is surrounded with glass windows which let the keen air through the crevices. I know how much time you spend in the library which to you is a very paradise."

The Bishop's stratagem of giving the books to St. John's College and borrowing them from their owners shared the fate of its originator. Before Fisher's beheading ". . . lest any conveyance might be made of his [Fisher's] goods remaining at Rochester, the King sent down Sir Richard Morrison of his private chamber with certain other commissioners to make a seizure of all his movable goods.

". . . They came into his library of books which they spoiled in most pitiful wise, scattering them in such sorte as was lamentable to behold. For it was replenished with such and so many kind of books as the like was scant to be found again in the possession of any one private man in Christendom. And of them they trussed up thirty-two great pipes; besides a number that were stolen away."

And so St. John's got none! This was probably the first, but assuredly not the last, great English library to be dispersed by Tudor zeal for learning. Before the end of the century the gathering together of the remnants of these libraries was mainly responsible for the immortal fame justly conferred on Sir Thomas Bodley.

XI - The Business of Death - The Poorest Bishopric

Just as infallibility is not sanctity, so too sanctity is not infallibility. It would therefore be no argument against our martyr's sanctity if his attitude towards the New Learning gradually changed as the thing itself grew from its early promise to its reality. Everything new that challenges what is old, finds in its lack of a past, an advantage over the old whose past is a field of wheat mingled with tares. Men like Linacre, Colet, More and Fisher were too devoted to the Church not to feel sympathy with a frank exposition of the internal ailments that threatened its life: yet the men of the New Learning who denounced in quasi-Ciceronian Latin every grade of the Church from the sole to the head were not themselves beyond suspicion. Even the thing they denounced as intellectual sloth masquerading as intellectual asceticism had certain justifiable intuitions. Some part of the opposition to the New Learning was because the new thing seemed twice-cursed: it came from Constantinople and it came through Florence. It reeked of the Photian schism and of the Medicean Machiavellianism. Moreover, its thinly veiled scorn for the Church's body of doctrine was not made authentic because the scorners had the capability or the hardihood to amend the Latin of Ambrose and Jerome.

27

It is to the credit of Erasmus that as early as 1524 he wrote: "Nothing is done by books against these men," the German Lutherans. These words were not only a denial of the inherent value of the printing press; but were almost a recantation by the man who had written twice as many books as any of his contemporaries.

Whilst in the Tower awaiting execution Fisher wrote these words to his Dominican sister, Catherine, warning her to prepare for death: "This provision [for a good death] therefore is most effectually to be studied, since this alone may profit without other; and without this none may avail. . . . And therefore delay it not as I have done, but before all other business put this first in surety which ought to be chiefest and principal business. Neither building of Colleges, nor making of sermons, nor giving of alms, nor yet any other manner of business shall help you without this."

Only a saint's humble delicacy of conscience saves this from being a grotesque exaggeration or an untruth, because no man in England had been longer or more devotedly about his Father's business. Even as he wrote he was hearkening to his Father calling him to a martyr's death; and he was running to obey his Father's call.

. . . " keen as a child across the grass."

One of the first and most natural effects of Master John Fisher being chosen as confessor to the King's mother, was his being chosen by the King for the bishopric of Rochester. It was a tragic year, in which Pope Julius II not only appointed Fisher to a bishopric but also granted Henry, Prince of Wales, a dispensation to marry his Spanish sister-in-law, Catherine of Aragon. The two papal acts seemed worlds apart. Yet they were so closely linked that they meant the martyrdom of the young Bishop.

For Fisher the appointment meant a new setting of his life but no new setting of his soul. What he was as a boy in the grammar school at Beverley; in the students' benches, or the professor's chair at Cambridge, he was still in the bishop's see at Rochester. The office which many of his contemporaries in Cambridge or Oxford would have looked on as a kingsway to success he looked upon as a charge and, either in substance or in effect, a temptation. We are told that in the few years that he had the confidence of Henry VIII, his sovereign offered him the sees of Ely or Lincoln. He declined to leave the poorest see in England for either of these rich sees, saying with an unwonted flash of humour: "I would rather keep my poor wife than marry the richest widow in England." His flash of wit was a grim, even if unconscious, comment on his king's attitude towards wedded love.

In reading the authentic records of how the Bishop bore himself in his bishopric we are perhaps a little surprised to find him praised for qualities which might be expected of any good bishop. But as there are times of general moral depression when the average layman's practice of the ten commandments demands heroic virtue, so there are circumstances when a bishop's fidelity to the ordinary duties of his office argues the saint. The contemporary biographers account these things of Fisher with no sense of narrating the average. Indeed they tell us that the fame of Fisher's sanctity went out from Rochester to the end of the Church.

There used to be a phrase which gave "the English Way" in matters of holiness, to wit: "Garden of the Soul Catholic." In reading what his biographer tell us of the holiness of Fisher we can hardly help recalling the phrase. Grafted upon a character that was sturdy almost to the point of severity, this holiness was in the common ways of Catholic life. It was based on the "three eminent good works" —the usual topic of Lenten preaching. The Bishop said Holy Mass often (though not daily) but always with devotion and with a skull placed on the altar. He said his Breviary faithfully. He was very reverent, with the national reverence, to the holy name of Jesus. His Master hidden in the Pyx before the High Altar drew him with such magnetic force that he had a hole made in the wall of the cathedral so that from the little room, with its bed of straw and mats, he might spend hours of fellowship with Him:

Qui nascens dedit socium.

His bodily mortifications were principally those of the Church. All Church fasts he kept even beyond the years when they are of obligation.

We are partially let into the secret of his strength, so violently contrasted with the weakness of his fellow-bishops, in the following naïve description: "The ordinary fasts appointed by the Church he kept very soundly; and to them he joined many other particular fasts of his own devotion, as appeared well by his soon thin and weak body, whereon though much flesh was not left, yet would he punish the very skin and bone upon his back. He wore commonly a shirt of hair; and many times he would whip himself in most secret wise."

Dear sensitive reader, do not shrink from this scholar, the friend of royalty who hastens from royal banquet tables and court mirth "to punish the very skin and bone upon his back." This quiet scholar from the Yorkshire moors is steeling himself to withstand Tudor Totalitarianism and to give a knight's chivalrous defence to an almost defenceless woman who was "England's Queen and England's guest."

Since stories of the Bishop's way with his poor flock are part of the heritage of English heroism, their realism shows us the soil on which Shakespeare grew: "Many times it was his chance to come to such poor houses as for want of chimnies were very smoky, so noisome that scant any man could abide in them. Nevertheless, himself would sit by the sick patient many times the space of three or four hours together in the smoke, when none of his servants were able to abide in the house, but were fain to tarry without till his coming abroad."

Once again, dear reader, do not tarry with the servants without, but abide if only for a moment in the smoke. There through the reek you will see not only a Bishop feeding his lambs, but a good shepherd learning from the patience of the poor, how meekly to lay down his life for his sheep.

Before the great storm broke which drove him from his peace at Rochester, some events made calls upon his learning or charity. Henry VII having died in 1509, it speaks of the place Fisher had won when this youngest and poorest of the Bishops was appointed to preach the panegyric in St. Paul's vast cathedral. It was the sermon not just of a courtier, but of an Englishman—a Yorkshireman—and a saint. England's aristocracy and England's royalty must have had conflicting emotions on hearing the metallic voice crying out: "Ah! King Henry, King Henry, if thou wert in life again many one that is here present now would pretend a full great pity and tenderness upon thee.

Ah! my lords and masters that have this world's wisdom, that study and employ your wits to cast and compass this world, what have ye of all this business but a little vanity? The spider carefully weaveth and joineth her web; but cometh a little blast of wind and disappointeth all together."

"This business." The phrase came back to him as he penned his last message in the death-quiet of the Tower. But whatever his lords and masters were set upon, this fearless panegyrist of the dead king was about the business of the King of Kings and Lord of Lords.

A few weeks later (29th June, 1509), in Westminster Abbey, he preached the panegyric of the great woman who was the mother of Henry VII and he could not forget that, with royal largesse, she had been something of a mother to the young Cambridge professor whom she had taken as Confessor. His words were so perfect a picture of this great and saintly Englishwoman that the preacher's canonisation may make them what they deserve to be made, a classic of English asceticism.

XII - Plain Speaking - Field of the Cloth of Gold - Defensor Fidei

In 1518 Cardinal Wolsey, Archbishop of York, was made Papal Legate for England. The Legatine Council which he summoned was chiefly remembered for the outspoken speech of the Bishop of Rochester. It was so characteristic an utterance that it throws light not only on the state of ecclesiastical and civil affairs but also on Fisher's attitude towards the state. Amongst other displays of Yorkshire frankness and reality is the following:

"In this trade of life neither can there be any likelihood of perpetuity with safety of conscience, neither yet any security of the clergy to continue, but such plain and imminent dangers are like to ensue as never were tasted or heard of before our days." (We have said that Fisher's life lacks miracles. But we are not so sure that it lacks prophecy; at least the prophecy of men who "discern the signs of the times.")

"For what should we exhort our flocks to eschew and shun worldly ambition, when we ourselves that are bishops do wholly set our minds to the same things that we forbid in them?

"What example of Christ our Saviour do we imitate, who first executed doing and after fell to teaching? If we teach according to our doing, how absurd may our doctrine be accounted! If we teach one thing and do another, our labour in teaching shall never benefit our flocks half so much as our examples in doing shall hurt them who can willingly suffer and hear with us, in whom (preaching humility, sobriety, and contempt of the world) they may evidently perceive haughtiness in mind, pride in gesture, sumptuousness in apparel, and damnable excess in all worldly delicacies? (England, like Jerusalem, did not lack its prophets; but it did not know the time of its visitation.)

"Truly, most reverend Fathers, what this vanity in temporal things worketh in you, I know not. But sure I am that in myself I perceive a great impediment to devotion, and so have felt for a long time. For sundry times when I have settled and fully bent myself to the care of my flock committed unto me, to visit my diocese, to govern my church, and to answer the enemies of Christ, straightways hath come a messenger for one cause or other, sent from higher authority, by whom I have been called to other business, and so left off my former purpose.

"And thus by tossing and going this way and that way, time hath passed, and in the meanwhile nothing done but attending after triumphs, receiving of ambassadors, haunting of princes' courts, and such like, whereby great expenses rise that might better be spent many other ways." (These ringing words approve their speaker a saint. But they also approve a great churchman and—pace Wolsey!—a great statesman).

One of these tinsel "triumphs" was perhaps even then in the making. History has called this triumph the Field of the Cloth of Gold. In its almost incredible magnificence and insincerity this elaborate kiss of Henry VIII and Francis I was the Judas greeting that ended the Ages of Faith.

In attendance upon Queen Catherine of England was the tall, gaunt figure of my Lord of Rochester, who kept his Yorkshire soul in touch with Realpolitik by saying Mass with a dead man's skull upon the altar!

Dear reader! has not some chill as of death swept over your soul as these two names—the hunted Queen and her knightly Bishop defender—are found for the first time side by side on that tragic page of history?

An almost parallel display was made by the King and his Chancellor, Cardinal Wolsey, on 12th May,

1521. In order to publish abroad the opposition to the new German heresies it was arranged to have a public burning of the heretical books at St. Paul's Cross.

Cardinal Wolsey presided. On his right were the Papal ambassador and the Archbishop of Canterbury. On his left were the Imperial ambassador and the Bishop of Durham. Round about the rest of the English hierarchy were seated. Fisher's learning and gift of English speech made him the preacher. A modern non-Catholic historian dubs it "A violent sermon;" no doubt through not having read it. It is a long, somewhat dry, theological argument on various opinions of the German Protestants. A kindred theme dealt from the mouth of Luther or Latimer would have been a flood of almost persuasive fallacy.

But no doubt the preacher at St. Paul's Cross was chosen less for his effect on Luther than on the select foreign representatives who could give a good account of the erudition and humanism and anti-Lutheran zeal to be found in Mary's Dowry. But St. Paul's Cross had not to wait long before it saw, as it were, the burned doctrines rise from the ashes!

The nine years between 1519 and 1527 were the saint's period of greatest literary activity. It began with a work, against Le Fevre, maintaining that there is one Mary Magdalene of the Gospels. Though the theme was not directly one of faith, nor indeed of Eastern acceptance, Fisher's book marked a stage in his literary history—if not in the humanistic movement. Le Fevre was one of the prominent humanists. Erasmus was so much the friend of the French humanist who championed the three Marys that he was somewhat nettled by the English humanist who championed one. Erasmus thought it disedifying that humanists could quarrel amongst themselves, whilst scholasticism was still unburied, though dead.

But Fisher's humanism was never such a devotion to style as lessened his greater devotion to truth; especially to any form of supernatural truth. For truth's sake he would willingly have suffered the loss of his friends, as indeed he suffered the loss of his life. The hiatus in the cordial relations between Fisher and Erasmus could only have been momentary or even mental. It may however have led to the Dutch humanist looking with more searching sight into the issues of the New Learning. Be that as it may, some time later on Erasmus had changed his ambiguous position between the old and the new by a very explicit declaration that the old was better.

The next few years saw his great work against Luther—(*Lutheranae Assertionis Confutatio*)—a work on St. Peter in Rome (against Willen)— a Defence of King Henry's book against Luther—a Defence of the Sacred Priesthood—a Defence of the Blessed Sacrament against Oecolampadius. With the exception of a Defence of Queen Catherine's marriage and three short treatises written in the

Tower the work on the Blessed Sacrament was the dramatic closing of his literary life. It was a life of prodigious literary activity. Even though it never reaches the peaks of genius, it shares, with his fellow northerner, the Venerable Bede, in a heroic power of taking pains. Fisher's first work amazed European readers by its research. It bore evidence to the double fact that he had perhaps the best episcopal library in Europe, and that, on the word of Erasmus, his library was haunted by its owner.

The Defence of the King's book against Luther belongs to the romance of literature. That the foul-mouthed German friar should draw an answer from the English king is almost a literary miracle of the first class. Doubts have been thrown on the king's authorship. But sound scholarship has ended these doubts.[1] Henry's youthful preparation for the priesthood gave him enough learning—and it never needed much—to refute Luther's challenge to the faith of Europe.

---

[1] Today one will find claims that Fisher is in fact the ghost writer of Henry's *Assertion in defense of the Seven Sacraments*, in places such as Wikipedia and not a few books. But this is altogether false, as scholarship in McNabb's day had shone. Firstly the Latin prose is foreign to Fisher's writing style, and more akin to Henry's and at times, that of Thomas More. Secondly, the *Assertio* mentions in no place Luther's doctrine of faith alone, which Fisher correctly understood was the basis of Luther's doctrine, and thus Fisher hammers that false doctrine not only in the sermon preached at St. Paul's Cross, but also in all of his writings against Luther. -Editor.

Luther's mastery of vituperation was shown in his answer to the King's answer. To Luther's foul-mouthings it was hardly fitting that an English sovereign should answer. No doubt the King's ecclesiastical champion was asked to undertake the King's further defence. Henry ought to have been grateful that the Chrysostom of his episcopate shielded him. History records but one exercise of that kingly gratitude, when His Majesty commuted Fisher's death sentence of drawing, hanging and quartering at Tyburn into beheading on Tower Hill.

XIII - "Both Blameworthy" - Crown vs. Church

A straw-in-the-wind that showed Fisher's strength of will was his attitude in the Convocation of 1523. The King's war with France and other royal extravagances necessitated a large subsidy from clergy and laity. Even the persuasion of the Speaker, Sir Thomas More, could barely wring it from the reluctant Commons. In Convocation the fruitless opposition was headed by Fisher, whose principles led him to think that the care of the poor rather than foreign wars was sound national policy. His opposition, though fruitless in a servile Convocation, was at least fruitful in begetting that kingly opposition which never lessened till Fisher's death.

And now, dear reader, I beseech you to beseech God for the seeing eye and the hearing ear. You are about to witness the relentless oncoming of two deaths: the death of a noble, chivalrous Englishman and the worse than death of England's oldest and most worshipful institution, the English Church. Until the last act of the last scene in this historic tragedy is played there is no shedding of blood; but only the summoning of royal Councils and royal servile parliaments, the issuing from the royal mind of the debased coinage of untruth, the promulgation of laws that made the crown rights of Christ to be sedition in English soil.

In witnessing the tragedy of a "Hierarchy that failed" be wary how and whom you judge. Alas! there are some judgments that are inevitable and vital. Yet in making them, ever remember the golden wisdom of Fisher's fellow-hero, Thomas More. Would God we were "All of the mind that every man thought no man so bad as himself; for that were the way to mend both them and us. Now they blame us, and we blame them; and both blameworthy. And either part more ready to find others' faults than mend their own."

Of first necessity in weighing and measuring the doings which gave the Sacred College of Cardinals its first canonized martyr a great historic fact must be borne in mind. Fortunately this fact can be stated in the words of one who did not share the faith of the martyr:

"That Rome exercised her spiritual power by the willing obedience of Englishmen in general, and that they regarded it as a really wholesome power, even for the control it exercised over secular tyranny is a fact which it requires no very intimate knowledge of early English literature to bring home to us.

"Who was 'the holy blissful martyr' whom Chaucer's pilgrims went to seek at Canterbury? One who had resisted his sovereign in the attempt to interfere with the claims of the papal Church. For that cause and for no other he had died: and for that cause and for no other, pilgrims who went to visit his tomb regarded him as a saint. It was only after an able and despotic king had proved himself stronger than the spiritual power of Rome that the people of England were divorced from their Roman allegiance; and there is abundant evidence that they were divorced from it at first against their will.[2]

This undeniable verdict of history may be summed up thus: There was never a struggle between the Church of England and the Church of Rome. But there was a long struggle, centuries old, between the Church of England and the Crown of England. Under Henry VIII the Crown won.

For two centuries after Pope Alexander III had blessed the standard of William, Duke of Normandy, the history of the struggle between Church and Crown centres round the great see of Canterbury.

---

[2] J. Gairdner: Lollardy and the Reformation in England, Vol. I, p. 5.

Lanfranc, Anselm, A'Becket took the attack of those Norman kings; whose ecclesiastical attitude was summed up in a contemporary proverb: "to fight a Pope, find a Norman." But King John's adroit move of making England a fief of the Pope seemed destined to dismantle Canterbury's defence against the Crown. Be that as it may, history records that after Innocent III had suspended Archbishop Stephen Langton for resisting King John no subsequent Archbishop of Canterbury was found in effective opposition to the Crown. Had Anselm or A'Becket been in the place of Warham or Wolsey the saddest pages of English history would have to be rewritten; perhaps as the most glorious.

It is then no little part of the tragedy of Fisher's life and death that although the Church of England had an Archbishop of Canterbury (Warham) whose conduct was above suspicion, and had even a papal legate, Cardinal Wolsey, whose civil statesmanship was almost without rival, the only effective opposition to the Crown's final attack on the Church of England came from the Bishop of the poorest of the English sees. *Beati pauperes!*

A new element had entered into this age-long struggle. Power or money had hitherto been the main object of the opposite forces. But with Anne Boleyn the main objective was transferred from the fourth and tenth commandments to the sixth: "Thou shalt not commit adultery."

Vincent McNabb, O.P.

The origin and the motives of Henry VIII's desire for a divorce are unknown to history. When historians tell us when and why Henry first thought of repudiating his wife who had borne him several children, history is passing into hazardous guess-work. But historians are hazarding less defensible guess-work when they endeavour to justify Henry's action by urging the purity or sincerity of Henry's motives. They do not see that if a good end does not justify bad means, still less do good means justify a bad end.

The first entry of Bishop Fisher owes its dramatic quality to the fact that it is only an official relation between an English diocesan bishop and the English representative of the Bishop of Rome. The Archbishop of York, who is also Lord Chancellor of England, Cardinal Wolsey, sends a letter to the Bishop of Rochester, and to other English diocesan bishops concerning the King's doubts about his marriage with Catherine of Aragon. The royal conscience was doubtful whether Catherine, who had wed Henry's brother, Arthur, could validly marry Henry, even when Pope Julius II had granted a dispensation.

Even if we were discussing this national question of the divorce from the side of Henry it would be irrelevant to discuss Henry's motives. But we are dealing with the divorce from the side of the theologian and a Bishop whose duty it was to consider only with justice.

43

Had Cardinal Wolsey read Fisher's sermons on the Penitential Psalms preached within a few weeks of his being appointed to the see of Rochester, the Cardinal would have foreseen the Bishop's fearless answer. There was almost a declaration of episcopal policy in these words of the preacher: "The office of correction belongeth first unto prelates and unto such as hath cure of souls. Which be set in this world by Almighty God as overlookers of the people. Unto whom also is commanded that they should shew to them their grievous offences.

"But they stand afar off and spare to say the truth. . . . Bishops be absent from their dioceses and parsons from their churches.

"No man will shew the filthiness of sin. All use bypaths and circumlocutions in rebuking them.

"We go nothing nigh to the matter. And so in the meanwhile the people perish with their sins. Which thing the prophet complaineth, saying: '*Et qui juxta me erant de longe steterunt,*' they that had cure of my soul stood afar from me. . . Prelates and parsons do not correct their misliving and shortly call them to amendment; but rather go by and suffer their misgovernance.

"What then? truly the soul, being glad of his destruction and in a manner running on his own bridle not helped by his friends—nothing cared for of the bishops and such as hath cure of souls—must needs come into the devil's power."

The young University-trained Bishop who said these things to his hearers said them because he meant them and meant to keep them. Later events showed that he could not at once keep them and his life. Yet they were kept!

Had these words been mere pulpit rhetoric they would have been a kind of sacrilegious burlesque. But the preacher's life and death made what would have been burlesque into tragedy, the quiet tragedy of a shepherd nerving himself to lay down his life for his sheep.

XIV - The Tragic Queen

Wolsey's demands to know Fisher's mind on the validity of Henry's marriage with Catherine was the turning-point in Fisher's life. As he could do nothing without doing it thoroughly, and as the matter concerned not only fundamental relations between the civil and ecclesiastical powers but also the fundamental question of a valid marriage the Bishop began his examination of the whole question.

A few months before his death an examination by King's commissioners occasioned the following self-revealing confession: "I am not certain of the number [of pamphlets, etc., he had written on the divorce], but I think seven or eight. The matter was so serious, both on account of the persons concerned and on account of the injunction given me by the King that I devoted more attention to examining the truth of it, lest I should deceive myself and others, than to anything else in my life."

No doubt his library, which Erasmus dreaded, with its many windows, was again haunted by the Bishop as in those happier days when the two humanists dwelt for a time under the same roof and were twin-brothers in the fellowship of books.

The first fruit of this long, deep study of the question was the Bishop's short answer to Wolsey's question. In a few downright words the clear-sighted student uttered the judgment which he never afterwards changed: "I am now thoroughly convinced that it can by no means be proved to be prohibited by any Divine law that is now in force, that a brother marry the wife of his brother deceased without children.

"If this is true—and I have no doubt that it is most certainly true—who can deny, considering the plenitude of power which Christ has conferred on the Sovereign Pontiff, that the Pope may dispense, for some very grave reason, from such a marriage?"

A scholar's and a saint's instinct had shown Fisher the issue in its ominous wholeness. It was a question not merely of a misunderstanding between a man and his legal wife, but of the power and therefore the divinity of Jesus Christ, who had instituted the Sacramental system and had organized the hierarchical order. From Rochester in Kent, his mind's eye saw the hamlet of Cana in

Galilee; and his mind's ear heard amid the Galilean hills "Thou art the Rock. And on this Rock I will build My Church!" This was not the exaggeration of fanaticism; but the accurate though distant focussing of faith.

In the July of 1527, Wolsey called on Fisher at Rochester on his way as special ambassador to France. By command of Henry, Wolsey discussed with Fisher the question of the royal divorce. The discussion must have been anguish to the scholar and Bishop whose writings had so stoutly defended the authority and dignity of the Popes. Fisher could look on Wolsey, the Papal Legate, only as the alter ego of Pope Clement VII. Yet, and here, dear reader, you must let me nerve myself to the tragedy by giving the words of Fisher's biographer (Fr. T. E. Bridgett, C.SS.R.):

"The King and Wolsey, by tricks and lies, sought to blind the man they most feared . . . The Cardinal went on to discuss the difficulties in the Bull of Dispensation granted by Julius II. But on this head he could not get much from the Bishop; who probably saw through the whole deceit."

The royal commissioners who made an inventory of the martyr's household belongings have noted: *"In the broad gallery old hangings of green say. An altar-cloth painted with green velvet and yellow damask. A St. John's Head standing at the end of the altar."* ! ! !

Before that head another John learned the craft of dying for the sanctity of the Great Sacrament.

And though no sign of the martyr's struggle with flesh and blood was ever witnessed by those around him, the "St. John's head standing at the end of the altar" may that night have heard, as the olive-grove once heard, a Hero praying that the chalice, almost too bitter for human lips, might pass away.

XV - Silence Veils Dissent

The martyr could not know that a chalice of even greater bitterness would be offered to his lips. As before, dear reader, let us offer it to our own shrinking lips with the words of the martyr's devoted biographer: "[The Pope, Clement VII, of the house of Medici] was threatened by the King, by Wolsey, by Parliament, by the King's agents, that to refuse the King's demand was to lose England for ever. He did at last refuse; saying that if England was to be lost it was better that it should be lost for justice than for injustice.

"But for nearly six years he dallied with the King; and protracted the suit by every possible means that was not criminal. It may be that, had he followed a different policy, and taken decided and strong measures from the beginning he would have served justice better and would have saved England to the Church. There were many who thought so then; and the Bishop of Rochester was among the number."

It needs but a loyal Catholic heart to feel in these words the deep tragedy of Fisher's death.

The matter of the divorce having been referred to Rome, Clement VII yielded to the King's demand that the case should be tried not in Rome but in England. Moreover, the Pope granted the demand that the verdict once given should be without appeal to Rome.

After four centuries and with the sight of a nation's change of faith it is easy to see the mistake committed by this deference to the King. Permission for a national Church to sit in judgment on the papal action of Julius II was almost a direct denial of papal authority. To Fisher's deep conviction of papal supremacy the appointment of Cardinal Campeggio as special legate and of Cardinal Wolsey to judge the validity of Henry's marriage must have been a mistake of the first magnitude.

Fisher's championship of truth and justice was gradually isolating him from the great ones in Church and State. But probably no isolation was so heavy a burden on his loyalty as that between himself and the Pope's special legate, Campeggio. Let the matter be told by the Saint's biographer: "It had always been held that even after a marriage had been validly contracted, if before its consummation one of the parties should make solemn profession in a religious order, the contract is dissolved. Some canonists were seeking in this fact a solution of Henry's difficulties. They argued that a marriage of doubtful validity (as they assumed this to be) might be set aside by papal dispensation, if Catherine would take a vow in some religious order.

"The scheme must have been entertained for a time by Campeggio.

"(In a letter to Rome) he writes: 'I do not despair of success in persuading the Queen to enter some religion. . . . As the Bishop of Rochester is in her favour I had a long interview with him on the 25th (October, 1528) and exhorted him to adopt this course for many reasons. When he left me he seemed to be satisfied with what I urged.'"

The Italian diplomat failed to interpret this gentlemanly silence of the Yorkshireman. It was not a silence that gave consent. It was a silence that veiled dissent; but quietly declined a useless wrangle of words.

Students of the psychology of martyrdom may one day make a profound analysis of the silence of Fisher and More. It was perhaps the most subtle achievement of their intelligence and heroism. For the moment Fisher's silence could be interpreted to mean an assent when the unofficial character of the assent was not jeopardising truth or justice. Perhaps Fisher's silence—always a defence of his duty—was never so heroic as when the lonely Queen Catherine complained that all she got from her counsellor the Bishop of Rochester was "to keep up her courage;" at the time when the Bishop was contemplating a defence of her which would cost him his life.

It is not part of this story of Fisher's life to describe the scene in Blackfriars' Hall, on 21st June, 1539, when the two Cardinals formally dealt with the Queen's appeal against the jurisdiction of this legatine Court. Shakespeare had generous matter of drama in the Queen's action of casting herself at the King's feet, reminding her disloyal husband that for twenty years she had been a loyal and loving wife. If the poet's account shows him to have been not always meticulous about his history, it shows him to have been one of the many Englishmen for whom the "new thing in religion"[3] had brought England into disgrace.

On the next day, 22nd June, 1529, the tall gaunt, quiet figure enters into the pageantry of this Tudor disgrace. He and a fellow-Bishop (Clarke, of Bath) appear at Blackfriars as proctors of the Queen. As Clarke had always proved himself to be Wolsey's man, the strong line taken by the two proctors was no doubt dictated by Fisher. They said that to prevent the King from falling into mortal sin they would defend the validity of the marriage, and they

---

[3]   Lest McNabb's use of the term "new things" be lost on modern readers, we add that in his time all his readers would have learned in their Latin schooling that in classical Latin *res novae* was an idiom for revolution. -Editor.

presented a writ of appeal, rejecting the two legatine judges as suspected.

Perhaps the future martyr did not see more in the day than that it was June 22nd, the feast of England's first martyr, St. Alban. Unless God had given him a revelation he could not see Tower Hill, June 22nd, 1535.

XVI - Rochester Speaks Out - A Parliament of Servants - Praemunire

The next sitting of the legatine Court, on June 29th, has been sketched for us by Cardinal Campeggio himself. The day after the Council he wrote to Salviati in Italy: "Yesterday the fifth hearing took place. Whilst matters were going on as usual owing to the Queen's contumacy the Bishop of Rochester appeared, and said in an appropriate speech that in a former hearing, he had heard the King's majesty discuss the cause and testify before all that his only intention was to get justice done, and to rid himself of the scruple he had on his conscience; inviting the judges and everyone else to throw light on the investigation of the cause.

"If on the offer and command of the King (said the Bishop) he did not come forward in public and manifested what he had discovered in the matter after two years and more diligent study he would be guilty.

"Therefore both in order not to procure the damnation of his soul, and in order not to be unfaithful to the King or to fail in doing the duty he owed to the truth, in a matter of such great importance he presented himself before his reverend Lordships to declare, to affirm and with forcible reasons to demonstrate to them that the marriage of the King and Queen can be dissolved by no power, human or divine. And for this opinion he declared he would even lay down his life.

"He added that the Baptist in olden times regarded it as impossible for him to die more gloriously than in the cause of marriage; and that, as it was not so holy at that time as it has now become by the shedding of Christ's blood, he could encourage himself more ardently, more effectually and with greater confidence to dare any great or extreme peril.

He indeed used many other fitting words, and in the end presented the book written by him on the subject . . . This affair of Rochester was unsuspected and unforeseen; and kept everyone in wonder. What he will do we shall see when the time comes. You already know what sort of man he is, and may imagine what is likely to happen."

Some little thought is needed to see the inwardness of this bold step. Even those who knew what sort of man and hero and saint Fisher was did not foresee the steps his heroism and holiness would take. But like his fellow-martyr, More (whom perhaps he consulted), every step was taken after profound thought. Against men like Henry and Wolsey and perhaps Cromwell, who were masters of Machiavellian diplomacy, the holiness of Fisher had to be supplemented by a skilful use of every privilege of law.

It will be noted that, in this scene, the Bishop of Rochester does not claim to be acting as the Queen's proctor. Having already informed the Court that the Queen had appealed to the Pope he could not and would not seem to represent the Queen as acknowledging the competence of the Court.

Yet if the Queen's proctor could not appear in the Court as Queen's proctor the Bishop of Rochester could appear and speak, and give evidence as Bishop of Rochester. Moreover, the matter of the divorce was grave enough for a diocesan Bishop to offer advice even if uninvited. Yet he offered advice not as uninvited but as commanded by the King for the quieting of the royal conscience.

This quiet stroke of law was unanswerable; and legally unpunishable. Henry's hypocritical appeal to his bishops to quiet his troubled conscience by a frank judgment on his marriage had overreached itself. It had allowed the most respected authority in the country to oppose the King's plans whilst carrying out to the letter the King's will.

To Henry and the astute flatterers whom Henry now favoured, it was clear that if Fisher's tongue and pen were to be silenced, some new point of fact or principle of law would have to be discovered or created!

Fisher's masterly self-control at this period is intellectual tragedy of the highest order. It is like an expert's most skilful and delicate rapier-play against a yokel's bludgeonings. He never loses his temper, whilst his enemies, who know his straightforwardness, are bewildered by the steps of this straightforwardness. Every step of theirs, even the most elaborately prepared, is met as if he had known it beforehand.

His relations with Queen Catherine must have perplexed the King and the King's men. Yet Fisher's action was so straightforward and accurate that it now appears obvious. Once he had acted as Queen's proctor in the legatine Court by appealing to Rome, he could only await Rome's decision. If Rome delayed—and an old proverb said *Roma Mora*—Fisher could only ask the Queen to be patient. Wisdom is seldom with haste. Moreover, any action he could take to hasten or influence Rome's decision would (firstly) be a breach of episcopal etiquette, and (secondly) a new source of weakness to the Queen's cause. Silence is said to be golden. But this silence of Fisher was no less steel than gold.

Towards the close of 1529, Henry summoned a Parliament. With the exception of a short session in 1523, it was the first Parliament for fourteen years.

But Henry had the wit to see that if he could get the Parliament he wanted he could get all—and that was much—that he wanted from Parliament. Hall the chronicler voices the common opinion of historians in the curt phrase: "most part of the Commons were the King's servants."

The first act of these "servants of the king" was to send to the King a Bill of Complaints against the clergy. No doubt they were proving themselves docile servants of the King by going on to pass and send to the Upper House a series of Bills encroaching on the legislative powers of the Church. When those Bills were sent to the Upper House the age-long struggle between the Crown of England and the Church of England was nearing its end.

That end would not have been reached if the Church of England had been given an Episcopate of men like Fisher; or even if a Fisher had taken Wolsey's or Warham's place as leader of the Episcopate.

What befell the Church of England in its struggle with a king who knew his aim and was not reckless but unscrupulous in attaining it, recalls the saying of Napoleon: "I would rather have an army of sheep led by a lion, than an army of lions led by a sheep." But indeed the English Episcopate had no leader—whether sheep or lion. In this matter of leadership the struggle against Henry VIII is in strong contrast with the struggle against his predecessor William Rufus. When Anselm, the scholar and saint, withstood Rufus at Rockingham he was, like Fisher, unsupported by the rest of the hierarchy. But Anselm was Archbishop of Canterbury. His Metropolitan see gave him the position of official leadership: his action counted to some extent for the action of the entire Episcopate. On the other hand, Fisher, Bishop of the poorest see in England, counted for no one but himself. Indeed his isolation from the policy of an Episcopate consisting mainly of expert jurists, took on the character of eccentricity. Such a characteristic deprived him of even the chance of making personal influence a substitute for official leadership.

When the Commons presented to the Upper House their Bills encroaching on the legislative power of the Church only Fisher's opposition was strong enough to have left a record in history. Saint that he was, his own rights, even as Bishop, were never primary, but only secondary and ancillary to his episcopal duties. If ever he sought the negative, necessary freedom from this or that enaction it was only for the positive freedom to fulfil this or that duty.

In appealing from Parliament and the King to the Pope, Fisher had the slender fellowship of the Bishops of Ely (West) and Bath (Clark). Henry's determination to be master of England's soul and body now manifested itself by the arrest and (short) imprisonment of all three. But in view of the past and future actions of West and Clark—who were on the panel of Queen Catherine's counsellors!—it is not certain whether their imprisonment was not part of the habitual Machiavellianism of the Crown. Fisher's imprisonment, though it probably meant no more than "being forbidden to break bounds" was on the side of the King and the Bishop the first grip in a deadly struggle.

Fisher's next trial of strength with the King and the King's men was in the Convocation of 1531. Wolsey's deposition from the Lord Chancellorship was followed by a prosecution under the Act of Praemunire, for having sought and exercised the office of Pope's legate in England. On his abject acknowledgment of his guilt the King confiscated Wolsey's vast wealth. The ease with which this ecclesiastical wealth could aid the royal finances suggested a more subtle and unheard-of device. All the clergy were prosecuted and convicted under the same Act of Praemunire for having admitted (as the King himself had admitted, and even welcomed!) Wolsey's legatine powers. It is needless to say that Henry was willing to show royal mercy for a large financial consideration.

The sordid tragedy of a spendthrift king wringing money by cut-purse tricks would find no place in this life of an Englishman who happened to be a saint if it did not lead to something more dramatic than financial roguery.

For the first time in the history of England, and indeed of the Church of Jesus Christ, a civil ruler set up the claim to be "the Supreme Head" of the Church in his kingdom. Something had gone wrong in the machinery of Church government when an entire national Hierarchy could make the royal claim a matter of several days' discussion. As far as we can judge from the only contemporary evidence there was but one member of the Hierarchy that had the foresight of the evils their Lordships' assent would ensure; and had outspokenness equal to his foresight. But what was the poorest diocesan in England against an insistent, unyielding, menacing sovereign and a hierarchy whose Archbishop's principle was *"Ira regis mors"*?[4] These timid shepherds did not see—and perhaps could not be expected to see that at its worst their choice was between their own death and the death of the Church of England. When they chose to live they had passed judgment that the Church of England should die.

The insight or courage lacking to his fellow-bishops was given in full measure to Fisher. Towards the end of the fateful deliberations he saw clearly that he was left alone to defend against the English Crown, the crown rights of Christ. A phrase used by the King's counsellors when bearing the King's message to the bishops was despairingly

---

[4] The Anger of the King is death. -Editor.

clutched at by Fisher in order to save defeat from being, what later it became, complete rout. These royal counsellors had said that the King claimed to be Supreme Head of the Church of England only *quantum per legem Dei licet*—as far as was allowed by God's law. Fisher urged and was at last successful in urging his timid brethren to accept the Supremacy only with this saving clause. It was the saint's last effort to rally the Church's defeated forces. Not on that day but in the end it was a tragic failure. The result was that Henry added one more to his innumerable breaches of faith and that Fisher has been accused of at least one breach of his wonted courage.

XVII - By Poison or Bullet - Mistress Anne's Concern - The Coming of Cromwell

The affair of the baulked poisoning is the nearest approach to a miracle in the saint's life.

On the 18th February, 1531, the Bishop tarried long in his library. If the matter of the Queen's divorce had been studied by him as nothing else in his life we may hazard a guess that this morning's study in the library was on the question of the royal Supremacy over the English Church. So long did he tarry that he bade his household take their midday meal whilst he would wait until evening.

As appeared later a certain Richard Roose put some poison into the food which the Bishop was to have eaten. It was such a deadly poison that all the household who ate of it were at the point of death. Two of the household and many of the poor to whom it had been given died.

It was impossible to keep the common folk from fastening the guilt of this crime on members of the Court circle—Mistress Ann Boleyn, for instance—who would have been the gainer by the Bishop's death. Perhaps in order to draw a false scent across the matter poor Richard Roose was thought worthy of a special Act of Parliament officially entitled 22 Henry VIII, ch. 9, condemning him of high treason! The chronicler of Grey Friars closes the grim story thus: "This year was a cook boilded in a cauldron at Smithfield, for he would have poisoned the Bishop of Rochester, Fisher. He was locked in a chair and pulled up and down with a giblet at divers times till he was dead."

No doubt procedure by Act of Parliament could be taken to show how highly the King valued the Bishop's life. But it also prevented cross questionings which might have proved awkward for some of the King's circle. The whole incident if not a sign of miraculous preservation is at least a curiosity of sixteenth century life and literature.

Poisoning having failed, the next attempt was made by gunnery. One day whilst Fisher was sitting in the study of his Lambeth house, a gun-shot tore through the roof of the house breaking and dismantling many of the tiles and rafters. Such havoc could have been made, not by a hand-gun, but only by some small piece of ordnance. The shot was found to come from a house on the other side of the Thames where dwelt the Earl of Wiltshire; father of Mistress Ann Boleyn! No Act of Parliament resulted from the gun-shot. With his usual wisdom, the Bishop, more concerned about his household than about himself, went back with them from Lambeth to what Erasmus thought to be the noisome atmosphere of the mud-flats of Rochester.

But the atmosphere about Henry's Court was of more subtle deadliness. Thus towards the close of 1531 when Parliament was summoned, the Lady Ann Boleyn sent special messengers to Rochester imploring the Bishop not to repeat the previous year's risk to his health by coming up to London for Parliament! The Lady's subsequent concern for Fisher's health—and indeed for Fisher's head—will enable students of psychology to form their own opinion upon the message sent from the royal Court to the Bishop's library.

The King and the King's men were dull judges of character if they thought to befool Fisher by an elaborate play-acting of lies. Every unworthy trick they played to entrap him shows their ignorance of the mind and soul of this quiet immovable Yorkshireman. Yet no act of his swerves from the high ideal of a gentleman or reveals a mind blind to the force of the royal assault against truth and right. Thus on the one hand he is still greatly anxious to further the cause of Queen Catherine.

Yet he knows that too public a support given to that cause will not further but endanger it. In the Queen's interest he keeps such an outward silence that even she begins almost to doubt of his interest. So subtly has he to work for justice in this new regal intriguing atmosphere of adultery and murder that he has to warn the Spanish Ambassador that neither of them must be known to exchange confidences by written or spoken word.

Yet Archbishop Warham was right, though cowed, when he said "*Ira regis mors.*" A king's anger is death. The King's verdict having been given that Fisher's tongue should be silenced it only remained for the King's clerical or lay jurists to work out evidence in accordance with the verdict; or to pass laws that would make the verdict English law!

The Bishop's action was in striking contrast with that of his fellow-bishops and that of his royal enemies. Whilst his fellow-bishops became more and more cowed until finally they consented to make no new regulations without the King's consent, Fisher became more and more bold until he dared to preach publicly against the Queen's divorce. So too whilst his enemies had to adopt almost secret plans for entrapping him, he used the publicity of his pulpit to denounce the royal action. That this bold stroke of preaching against the divorce was not at once followed by the preacher's arrest and condemnation is a historic fact which historians have not yet seen in its full significance. First of all it is a sign that in spite of widespread fear of Henry's cruelty there was an equally widespread condemnation of his policy. Secondly, this widespread sympathy with the opinion preached publicly by Fisher was known and feared by the royal party; who, for the moment, felt themselves unprepared to meet it in open battle or at least on equal terms.

But More's resignation of the Lord Chancellorship, and the appointment of Audley had given greater freedom of action to Henry's new servant Cromwell, whose plans were not likely to be thwarted or even delayed by any disturbance of conscience. Cromwell's Machiavellian studies in their native Italy were soon to bring his Italian-trained finesse into deadly conflict with the Yorkshireman who stood for what was best in English love of truth and justice. How Cromwell finally contrived to obtain a conviction against the Yorkshireman by force of law is a part of the great Fisher tragedy which smacks not a little of the burlesque.

Here is the story in sufficient outline. A poor serving maid, Elizabeth Barton, in Aldington, Kent, was reputed to have visions and trances. When she was sixteen years of age her spiritual advisers counselled her to enter the Benedictine convent at Canterbury. No doubt they thought it the safest place for a reputed visionary at such a susceptible age.

When the King began to seek the divorce the "Holy Maid of Kent"—for such was she called—naturally had alleged revelations concerning the unlawfulness of the King's project. Her belief in the truth of her visions was so great that she even accepted an invitation to speak personally to the King !

To the ordinary Englishman of the time, Elizabeth Barton was a good-living woman who thought she heard heavenly voices; but whether she did hear them and whether if she heard them they were heavenly, cleric and lay-folk were divided. Now what was to the ordinary Englishman hardly more than a faintly uncommon piece of spiritual gossip was to the subtle mind of Cromwell an opportunity for netting a complete catch of the men who were thwarting the royal will to marry Ann Boleyn. The Holy Maid by herself would hardly have been worth a page of parchment. But almost every major opponent of the King's project, including the maid's diocesan Bishop of Rochester, could be caught in the net.

A Bill of Attainder convicted of treason the Maid, two Benedictines, two Franciscans and two parsons. Tyburn tree saw them all duly hanged, drawn and quartered on 2 I st April, 1534.

But this group attainted of treason was not so important to the King as the second group attainted of misprision of treason. This included Fisher, the

Queen's undaunted champion, and Abell, the Queen's chaplain (a beatified martyr), and others.

XVIII - A Noble Letter - The Crown Wins

Our readers may well be spared the details of a successful Cromwellian plot to give legal sanction to the imprisonment and consequent silencing of the tongue that could not be bribed or bullied into injustice or untruth. The sordid story is redeemed by some noble letters of Fisher to the King and the Lords and to Cromwell.

One of them deserves to take its place in the literature of England and of liberty by the side of Johnson's letter to Lord Chesterfield. But our readers themselves shall adjudge its worth:

". . . After my right humble commendations I most entirely beseech you that I no further be moved to make answer unto your letters. For I see that mine answer must rather grow into a great book, or else be insufficient, so that ye shall still thereby take occasion to be offended and I nothing profit.

"But I perceive that everything I writ is ascribed either to craft, or to wilfulness, or to affection or to unkindness against my sovereign; so that my writing rather provoketh you to displeasure than it furthereth me to any point concerning your favour which I most effectually covet.

"Nothing I read in all your long letters that I take any comfort of but the only subscriptions wherein it pleaseth you to call you my friend; which undoubtedly was a word of much consolation unto me. And therefore I beseech you so to continue and so to show yourself unto me at this time.

"In two points of my writing methought ye were most offended and both concerned the King's Grace. That one was where I excused myself by the displeasure that His Highness took with me when I spake once or twice unto him of like matters. That other was where I touched his great matter.

"And as to the first methink it very hard that I might not signify unto you such things secretly as might be most effectual for mine excuse.

"And as to the second, my study and purpose was specially to decline, that I should not be straited to offend his Grace in that behalf. For then I must needs declare my conscience; the which (as then I wrote) I would be loth to do any more largely than I have done.

"Not that I condemn any other men's conscience. Their conscience may save them; and mine must save me.

"Wherefore, good Master Cromwell, I beseech you for the love of God, be contented with this mine answer, and to give credence unto my brother in such things as he has to say unto you.

"Thus fare you well.

"At Rochester, the 31st day of January [1534].

St. John Fisher

"By your faithful headman.

"Jo. ROFFS."

In every anthology of English literature this courteous letter should find a place, if only for its delicate reference to Cromwell's subscription as "friend." But a no less honourable place should be found for it in every anthology of the literature of human liberty. The old, dying Bishop is one of freedom's unyielding gladiators.

He is fighting, in our stead, not only for man's Freedom of Speech, but for that almost more necessary right, a man's Freedom of Silence! The cowards and cads who were the then masters of Englishmen and Englishwomen, first of all compelled their victims to speak and then were prepared to hang, draw and quarter them for having spoken! Against this totalitarian frightfulness no one stood out so effectively as the old dying Bishop of Rochester. And nowhere was his pen guided to such perfect expression of a human being's inalienable and supreme right as in the phrase: "Not that I condemn any other men's conscience. Their conscience may save them; and mine must save me." To keep that one phrase alone we might be content to lose all else that Fisher wrote.

Though the Bill of Attainder convicted Fisher of misprision of treason, the sentence of imprisonment and confiscation of goods was delayed until another Act was passed which could change misprision of treason into treason. Once convicted of high treason, Fisher's unconquerable tongue could be silenced, not in a dungeon but in death!

It was always the marriage that mattered. Were we writing the story of Henry it would be necessary to let the readers feel the influence of Ann Boleyn in these acts of royal absolutism. But in this story of Fisher they are necessary only as a Salome background to the beheadal of a prophet.

Ann's secret marriage with Henry on January 25th, 1533, and the birth of Elizabeth on September 7th, had made it necessary to legitimatize the marriage and the offspring. This again made it necessary to repudiate the power and authority of the Pope who might be counted upon to uphold the dispensation granted by his predecessor. An Act of Succession was hurried through Parliament. The offspring of the marriage with Ann Boleyn were declared legitimate and the right of Succession was limited to the issue of this marriage. To oppose this succession was declared to be high treason; to speak against it was declared to be misprision of treason.

The fine flower of Tudor Totalitarianism is now first seen in the clause empowering the King to oblige all his subjects to take an oath to keep the provision of the Act: "And if any persons being commanded by authority to take the said oath . . .

obstinately refuse that to do, in contempt of the Act, they become guilty of misprision of treason."

Parliament had been so intelligently planned and packed that the terms of an oath which has meant centuries of national dismemberment were left to a group of the King's men. The Machiavellian touch of absolutism was guaranteed by including in the group the King's Secretary, Cromwell.

Several forms of oath were tried and rejected. But the substance of these forms was the repudiation of any foreign authority, prince or potentate. This was a designed and effective repudiation of England's nine-century acknowledgment of papal authority. The King's thoroughness in ill-doing might have taught the Hierarchy that force alone could meet force. Compromise even when resting on the King's promise was only organized defeat. Dear reader! imagine, if you can, how much is the England of Anselm and A'Becket unsaying when, with one exception, the bishops take oath in these words: "From this day forward I shall swear, promise, give or cause to be given to no foreign potentate, NOR YET TO THE BISHOP OF ROME, whom they call the Pope, any oath or fealty, direct or indirect. . . . I profess the Papacy of Rome not to be ordained of God by Holy Scripture," etc.

Had Fisher been in London instead of being ill at Rochester there is little reason to think the bishops' cowardice would have turned hero. Though the bishops realized that his advice was always that of wisdom and holiness, his influence was like that of a sensitive conscience which cannot be stifled and will not be obeyed.

On March 23rd, Pope Clement VII ended the matter of this divorce by pronouncing the validity of Henry's marriage with Catherine. On Holy Saturday, April 4th, the news reached England. The Supreme Head of the Church of England ordered the preachers on Easter Sunday to say their worst against the Pope. Rochester Cathedral saw its heroic saintly Bishop celebrate for the last time on Easter Sunday. Easter alleluias were in sad contrast with the sorrow cast over the Bishop's household by a message from Archbishop Cranmer summoning Fisher to Lambeth in order to take the oath.

Like his Master who went forward with haste towards the city of His crucifixion, Fisher found strength enough in his will to set out for London the next day, Easter Monday. The only account of those last tragic hours gives us but the old quiet John Fisher we have always known.

"He has grown; he has not changed. His body has grown weaker; it may even fail to reach London. His soul has grown stronger; it will soon be strong enough and "young enough to die."

But though there is a good deal of mourning and weeping round him he is quietly calming them in such a wonted way that the eye-witnesses have no dramatic act or word of his to record. There is no dramatic meeting or leave-taking in the Minster. The shepherd goes to give his life for his sheep as silently and almost as shyly as the Master Shepherd stole at midnight into the shadows of a stable.

He had little or no time to make ready. Yet he had time enough to see that his household and his beloved poor were the richer by his going. Even Michael House, Cambridge, had a noble gift of £100. His memory of it and of his happy boyhood days in it belong to the unknown romance of Fisher's silent heart.

One incident on the road to London deserves to be rescued from the obscurity of its unimpassioned record. We are told that after a journey of some miles "he came to a place called Shooters Hill, at the top whereof he rested himself and descended from his horse . . . he caused to be set before him such victuals as were hither brought for him . . . and there dined openly in the air."

Again, there is no gesture—there is only a meal in the open air, as if His Lordship was on picnic. There is no dramatic turning towards Rochester, his beloved see, with a bishop's blessing. Yet, at least one lover of John Fisher, Yorkshireman, wonders whether a bishop's heart was not then breaking. When he reached London at last, it was night: *Erat nox!*

On Monday, 13th April, the Bishop went from his house in Lambeth Marsh to Lambeth Palace, where the Royal Commissioners sat to administer the oath of Succession. These Commissioners were Cranmer, Audley, the Lord Chancellor, Benson, Abbot of Westminster, and Cromwell, the King's Secretary.

More, the fellow-champion and fellow-martyr, has left us an undying record of that day so fateful in England's history. A group of priests and Bishop Fisher had been summoned to take the oath. As More was the first to be called and had refused the oath he had the honour to be the first English subject officially to resist Tudor Totalitarianism.

In a letter written a few days later to his daughter Margaret Roper, he has described the scene with his own mastery of words: "When I refused to swear . . . I was commanded to go down into the garden. And thereupon I tarried in the old burned chamber that looketh into the garden, and would not go down because of the heat.

"In that time I saw Master Dr. Latimer come into the garden and there walked he with divers other doctors and chaplains of My Lord of Canterbury. And very merry I saw him, for he laughed and took one or twain about the neck so handsomely that even they had been women I would have weened he had waxen wanton.

"After that came Master Dr. Wilson (once a royal chaplain) forth from the Lords and was with two gentlemen brought by me and gentlemanly sent straight unto the Tower.

"What time my lord of Rochester was called in can I not tell. But at night I heard that he had been before them, but where he remained that night and so forth till he was sent hither (i.e., the Tower) I never heard.

"I heard also that Master Vicar of Croydon (Roland Phillips) and all the remnant of the priests of London that were sent for were sworn . . . that Master Vicar of Croydon either for gladness or for dryness or else that it might be seen *Quod ille erat notus Pontifici* (that he was known to the High-priest) went to my lord's buttery bay and called for drink and drank *valde familiariter.*"[5]

A warm spring day in mid-April—an English garden and by the banks of the Thames—almost the world's fairest sight. What a setting for a murder plot! This undying picture with its quiet irrepressible fun we owe to the undying wit of the merry Londoner who, after nights of agony, met death and met it with a laugh.

Fisher's way of meeting death was different because he had a different part to play. Being conscious that he was a shepherd who had to lay down his life for his sheep and indeed to lead his sheep into the shamble of death, he had to show something of the stolidity of a commanding officer in the moment of greatest danger.

---

[5] On exceedingly friendly terms. -Editor.

But that commanding officer is no longer the tall hale Yorkshireman who loved hare-coursing on his beloved moors. A thumbnail sketch of him is given by one of the new King's-men whose pity could be moved only by the extreme of woe. Roland Lee, the lately consecrated Bishop of Lichfield, writes to the "man who mattered," i.e., Cromwell: "Truly the man is nigh gone, and cannot continue long unless the King and the Council are merciful to him; for the body cannot bear the clothes on the back."

It was then a dying body but an undying will and an alert mind that went before the Archbishop and his three fellow-commissioners. When the oath was offered to him he asked that he might see it and might have a little time to read it. That same morning the same room in Lambeth Palace had heard the same request by More. But whereas More had taken but a few moments to verify his conviction that the oath was against his conscience, Fisher asked and obtained a few days for examining the matter.

Perhaps the manner in which Fisher was asked to take the oath suggested his caution. Cranmer as Archbishop of Canterbury was, though in a limited sense, Fisher's ecclesiastical superior. Moreover, in asking Fisher to take the oath the Archbishop was able—and careful!—to tell him that it had been taken by all the lords, temporal and spiritual. To refuse would look like obstinacy born of pride.

But Fisher knew that in these matters of spirituality, the truth is not decided by a majority vote even of a national hierarchy.

During the days of his reprieve many of his friends knowing the King's mind came to bid him farewell. One day he was visited by two fellows of St. John's College, Cambridge, which Margaret of Richmond and he had founded. Cranmer had amended the statutes of the College. But these amendments needed the approval of Fisher as the executor of Lady Margaret. The two visitors asked the Bishop to put his seal on the statutes. He replied that he would set his seal when he had re-read them. They pleaded that he might soon be for prison. He said, "I will read them in prison." They answered: "Nay, that will not come to pass." Then said he: "Let God's will be done; for I will never allow under my seal that thing which I have not well and substantially viewed and considered."

A story is told that during the process of canonizing St. Thomas Aquinas it was reported to the Pope that there were no miracles wrought by St. Thomas. Whereupon the Pope replied, "St. Thomas has wrought as many miracles as he has written articles in his Summa." Perhaps in days to come when someone objects that Fisher's life lacks all miracle, a lover of this great immovable commanding officer in the day of a nation's defeat will recall this incident of the martyr's refusal to set his seal on anything he had not considered.

XIX - Refusal to Sign - The Machiavellian Touch

On Tuesday, April 21st, 1534, he was again before Cranmer and the other Commissioners at Lambeth Palace. In a letter to Cromwell written from prison in the Tower on December 22nd of the same year, Fisher's own truthful pen describes what took place: "I must beseech you good Master Secretary to call to your remembrance that, at my last being before you and the other Commissioners for taking of the oath concerning the King's most noble succession, I was content to be sworn unto that parcel concerning the succession.

"And there I did rehearse this reason which I said moved me. I doubted not but the prince of any realm with the assent of his nobles and commons might appoint for his succession royal such an order as was seen unto his wisdom most according. And for this reason I said that I was content to be sworn unto that part of the oath as concerning the succession.

"This is very truth as God help my soul at my most need.

"Albeit that I refused to swear to some other parcels because that my conscience would not serve me so to do." These parcels to which he would not, and never did, swear, contained the rejection of the papal authority to decide amongst other things, the validity or invalidity of a marriage; and to dispense with impediments which were not of the natural law.

That day when the old bishop "whose body could not bear clothes on his back," refused to deny the authority of the Pope, the See of Peter was beginning to receive perhaps its greatest authentication by blood, and the illustrious College of Cardinals was preparing to honour its first canonized martyr.

The contemporary manuscript life says almost laconically ". . . upon which answer he was sent straightway to the Tower of London . . . and this was done on Tuesday the 21st of April, in the year of our Lord God, 1534, and the 25th year of the King's reign, being the last day of his reign for that year."

And thus the Defender of the Faith closed his first royal Jubilee !

Cromwell's experience as a house-and land-agent was not likely to overlook the fact that misprision of treason carried with it not only imprisonment but confiscation of goods. Fisher was in the Tower on Tuesday, 21st April—Cromwell's men were in Rochester making an inventory of the Bishop's goods on Monday, 27th. The Record Office still contains the "Inventory taken, 27 April, 26 Hen. VIII, of the goods and household implements of the Bishop of Rochester being in the said house, to the use of the King."

In recalling what Robinson Crusoe saved from his wreck, Mr. Chesterton has pointed out the drama of a list of things that a man has; and especially such things as a man has in an hour of stress. The inventory of Bishop Fisher made within a week of his imprisonment in the Tower is part of the tragedy of his life and death. Probably few inventories of men committed for treason or misprision of treason contains so many entries of "old" *implements.* Thus: "In his own bed chamber . . . a celer and tester of *old* red velvet *nothing worth,*" (we hazard a guess that he found it there when he first slept there as Bishop, thirty years before) ". . . a stool with an *old* cushion upon it.

"In the chapel at the end of the south gallery . . . 2 pieces of *old* velvet.

" In the broad gallery. . . . *Old* hangings of green say. Old carpets of tapestry. . . . 2 *old* sarcenets.

" In the old gallery. Certain *old* books pertaing to divers monasteries."

Dear reader! Would you not like to know what were these old books? The men sent down to list the King's loot could not be expected to recognize in them anything but that they were old like the hanging "of green say" in the chapel, or "the celer and tester of old red velvet nothing worth" in the Bishop's own bedroom.

Again "In the little chamber next the same chapel. Hangings of *old* painted cloth—a great looking glass *broken.* An *old* folding bed.

"In the parlour, 5 pieces of very *old* green verdour ... a very *old* carpet in the window."

It reads like a list of things on a stall in Islington Market. Yet it is the authentic inventory of a scholar and royal chaplain who by the favour of the Holy See was a Bishop and Cardinal, and by the grace of God was a saint and a martyr.

Three items lift a little the veil of silence covering the Bishop's ways of holiness. His own bed-chamber contained "A bedstead with a mattress, a counterpoin of red cloth lined with canvas."

But "In Master Wilson's chamber a feather bed . . . In the cook's chamber a feather bed and bolster."

Only a mattress in the Bishop's poor room; but a feather bed for his butler and cook!

A further contrast must be left to the intuition of the reader: "An inventory ... of the goods ... of the Bishop of Rochester ... to the use of the King.

"In the broad gallery . . . A ST. JOHN'S HEAD standing at the end of the altar"!

But the inventory in the Record Office fails to note a further "household implement;" perhaps because it could hardly have been "to the use of the King."

In the oratory where he prayed most there stood a coffer securely locked. The household could tell nothing of it, save that it must keep something precious because its owner guarded it so jealously.

From this account of it the Commissioners concluded that they might incur the royal displeasure if they opened it secretly. Thereupon they summoned a number of witnesses to guarantee that the said Commissioners had nowise tampered with royal treasure.

Gignitur ridiculus mus![6] When the coffer was broken open the royal loot consisted of "not the gold and silver which they looked for, but a shirt of hair, and two or three whips wherewith he used full often to punish himself."

How often is tragedy heightened by burlesque!

Roper, husband of Meg More, has characteristic stories to tell of More's arrival in the Tower. But Fisher's arrival is fitly recorded with characteristic brevity. "Then said my Lord of Rochester. . . I do absolutely refuse the oath," upon which answer he was sent straightway to the Tower of London . . . and this was done on Tuesday the 21st of April, in the year of our Lord God, 1534 and the 25th year of the King's reign."

He was not alone in his new home. Already Nicolas Wilson, a King's chaplain, had begun the way of a martyr which he was to abandon after three years. The Beauchamp Tower had admitted

---

[6] "A ridiculous mouse is born." McNabb is making an allusion to the Roman Poet Horace's line: "Partuerint Montes, et nascentur ridiculus mus," (Ars Poetica, 139) meaning great labors that bring forth nothing. -Editor.

81

Fisher's fellow-champion, More, on Friday the 17th. And perhaps in the same Beauchamp Tower was there another martyr, Bd. Thomas Abel,[7] who had been a staunch defender, counsellor and chaplain of Queen Catherine.

As Fisher was confined in the bell tower he was a near neighbour of More, with whom during the fourteen months of his imprisonment he exchanged some five or six letters. In the end these letters meant an addition to their writers' punishment, if also to their consolation.

Now that the gate of the Tower has closed upon our hero, we can try to see what is happening. An old Englishman, who has been the loyal and even loving servant of two kings, is in prison on a charge of disloyalty. He is reckoned an enemy of his birth-land because he still gives spiritual obedience to that papal authority which gave his birth-land its religion, its civilization, and even its political unity.

But for the moment England is in the hands of a king who has been called "A spoiled child and a spoiled priest;" and this king is in the hands of passions that are uncontrolled by the divine

---

[7] Abel wrote a treatise in Latin which defended the Queen's case in a very public manner. He published it abroad, though he had been sent by Henry to canvass in favor of the divorce. A copy of the work is still extant among Henry's possessions, which bears an inscription written by Henry himself on the title page, in Latin, which says: "the whole basis of the case is false." -Editor.

precepts: "Thou shalt not commit adultery. Thou shalt not steal."

At the side of the king is an Englishman almost without parallel in the history of England: Thomas Cromwell. Contrasted with Henry and, still more, contrasted with Fisher, he is almost a phenomenon without antecedents. Though he seems to be the creation of his circumstances he takes care that circumstances never find him without a plan.

Some of these plans have come down to us in the "Remembrances" which were seized when he was arrested on his death-charge.

The painstaking unscrupulousness of the English Machiavelli can be felt in the following "Remembrance" which Cromwell wrote in his notebook in these days of administering the oath. It is in the British Museum, catalogued Titus B. 1, 463: "Who shall be sent to the French king and what instructions he shall have. To cause the statutes touching the Pope's authority and the King's succession to be abridged that the effect of them may be declared to the French King.

"To approach the most assured and substantial gentlemen in every shire to be sworn of the King's Council, with orders to apprehend all who speak or preach in favour of the Pope's authority.

"To have substantial persons in every good town to discover all who speak or preach thus.

"To have the Act of Succession openly proclaimed that the people may not make themselves ignorant thereof. Whoever shall offend to be ordered according to the same Statute.[8]

"The beacons throughout the realm to be repaired. Letters to be written to persons having fortresses near the coast to see them ordered; and the artillery and munitions put in readiness and cleansed. The Master of the Ordnances to be warned to see to the ordnance and munitions put in order. To call upon Wm. Gonston, Spert, and others having charge of the King's ships to have them repaired.

To send for my Lord Chancellor to-morrow and for my lord of Wiltshire (father of Anne Boleyn).

"To appoint preachers throughout the realm to preach the Gospel and true word of God. To send for my lord of Canterbury.

"To see the King's chequer roll for the appointing of assured gentlemen and yeomen in every shire and good town as aforesaid.

"To send a copy of the Act of the King's succession to the Princess Dowager (Queen Catherine) and the lady Mary, with special commandment that it may be read in their presence and their answer taken.

"A deputy to be sent into Ireland with all speed to set a stay there.

---

[8] After this proclamation no one could plead ignorance; and thereby avoid the penalties of the Act.

"Letters to be sent to the officers in Wales to have regard to these ports and gentlemen and yeomen to be appointed to apprehend any Papists who preach, etc., to the advancement of the authority of the Bishop of Rome.

"The Scotch ambassador to be put off till Tuesday.

"General musters to be made through the realm if it is the King's pleasure."

It is clear that the man who could continue and carry out this programme of civil, military, naval and ecclesiastical policy was not a slave but a master of circumstances.

His imprisonment of Fisher (and More) was not a consequence of the Act of Succession; but almost its motive. By a clever stroke of unscrupulousness the Act of Succession with its Oath of Succession had enabled Cromwell and Henry to turn the Oath of Succession into an Oath of Royal (as against Papal) Supremacy. Hence Fisher and More, who did not refuse the Oath of Succession but did refuse the Oath of Supremacy, were judged guilty of an offence created by no law. Yet by a device which threw a cloak of law over the royal iniquity the two leaders of clergy and laity were safely silenced in the Tower.

It was the first time that Catholics—clergy and laity—were called upon to suffer officially for the supremacy of the Pope. For them and for all the martyrs of Henry's reign, this is their unique honour that they died solely for the Holy See.

The later martyrs died not only for the Holy See but mainly for the Real Presence of Jesus in the Holy Sacrament and Sacrifice of the Altar.

Cromwell's plan with Fisher was an alternative. He would first attempt to win over the Bishop. But if the Bishop would not yield to the King's pleasure he must incur the King's displeasure to the full.

Only the outlines of this plan in its execution have been left to us. The Bishop was to be attacked in body and mind.

Even though confinement in the upper room of the Bell Tower did not mean an underground dungeon, nor the rack, it must have meant for Fisher an almost intolerable bodily discomfort. It was not a man in the full strength of mid-life that went into this upper room of the Bell Tower. It was an old man who swooned several times on his short journey from Rochester to Lambeth; and who was so visibly ailing that even Rowland Lee spoke of his back as unable to bear his clothes.

Only once in the course of his fourteen months of confinement did he leave the precincts of the Tower, perhaps even the narrower circuit of his cell—when a few days before his death he was led to Westminster Hall to be tried.

XX - "My Duty Saved Unto God - A Bishop in Rags - Writing in the Tower

A letter of the Bishop, on 22nd December, 1534, will let the reader into some of the secrets of the Bishop's martyrdom. It is a letter written to Cromwell as Secretary of the King, and written by command. So great a light does it throw on the character of the writer and the circumstances of his imprisonment that it shall be given in full."After my most humble commendations whereas ye be content that I should write unto the King's Highness, in good faith I dread me that I can not be too circumspect in my writing, but that some word shall escape me wherewith His Grace shall be moved to some further displeasure against me, whereof I would be very sorry. For as I will answer before God. I would not in any manner of point offend His Grace—my duty saved unto God whom I must in everything prefer.

"And for this consideration I am full loth and full of fear to write unto His Highness in this matter. Nevertheless and if, then, I conceive that it is your mind that I shall so do, I will endeavour me to the best that I can.

"But, first, here I must beseech you, good Master Secretary, to call to your remembrance that at my last being before you, and the other Commissioners for taking of the oath concerning the King's most noble succession I was content to be sworn unto that parcel concerning the succession. And there I did rehearse this reason which I said moved me. I doubted not but the Prince of any realm with the consent of his nobles and commons might appoint for his succession royal such an order as was seen unto his wisdom most according. And for this reason I said that I was content to be sworn unto that part of the oath as concerning the succession.

"This is very truth; as God help my soul at my most need. Albeit I refused to swear to some other parcels because that my conscience would not serve me so to do.

"Furthermore, I beseech you to be good master unto me in my necessity; for I have neither shirt nor suit but that be ragged and rent to shamefully. Notwithstanding, I might easily suffer that if they would keep my body warm.

"But my diet; also, God knoweth how slender it is many times. And now in mine age my stomach may not away but with a few kinds of meats, which if I want I decay forthwith and fall into coughs and diseases of my body; and cannot keep myself in health.

"And, as our Lord knoweth, I have nothing left unto me for to provide me better, but as my brother of his own purse layeth out for me to his great hindrance. Wherefore, good Master Secretary, oftsoons I beseech you to have some pity upon me and let me have such things as are necessary for me in mine age and especially for my health.

"And also that it may please you, by your high wisdom, to move the King's Highness to take me unto his gracious favour again, and to restore me unto my liberty out of this cold and painful imprisonment whereby ye shall find me to be your bedesman[9] for ever unto Almighty God, Who ever have you in His protection and custody.

"Other twain things I must also desire upon you. That one is that it may please you that I may take some priest within the Tower by the assignment of Master Lieutenant to hear my confession against this holy time. The other is that I may borrow some books to stir my devotion more effectually these holy days for the comfort of my soul. This I beseech you to grant me of your charity.

"And thus Our Lord send you a merry Christmas and a comfortable to your heart's

"At the Tower, the 22nd day of December."

"Your poor Bedesman,

" Jo. ROFFS."

Dear reader! By all canons of art this letter belongs to the noble literature of life; and, indeed to the nobler literature of death. Now that you have read it once, read it once again, lest you be caught only by the quiet music of its sixteenth century

---

[9] In Early Modern English, *bedesman* meant someone living on alms by the support of a benefactor in exchange for prayers. -Editor.

prose; whilst still untouched by the music of a soul throbbing with a humble love of God and men.

1. If you are students of English history—or rather, if you are spectators of the drama of English history, this letter of Fisher the prisoner to Cromwell will stand in violent contrast with another letter a few years hence of Cromwell the death-sentenced prisoner to the King whom he had served better than he had served God.

There is an old saying that "A tyrant is a coward." Men like Cromwell can sometimes find a place in history amongst the strong; when their show of strength is but a callousness or cruelty which is but the self-defence of cowardice.

Fisher's letter to the King's Secretary is noble enough for a king to have written. Master Secretary's petition for the King's mercy is abject in its cringing.

2. Take notice of the Bishop's noble phrase "my duty saved unto God whom I must in everything prefer." Fisher was not primarily concerned with his liberty as an Englishman, because such liberty is not primary. But because his liberty as an Englishman was bound up with his liberty as a Catholic his fight for the right to fulfil his duty to God enrols him as a martyr for liberty. He is not only an English martyr but an English patriot. By right of blood he is brother to those first martyrs who overcame the Roman tyranny not by taking life

but by giving it. More's and Fisher's way of redemption was not by revolution but by sacrifice.

3. Behind Master Secretary's great concern that Fisher shall write a letter for the eyes of the King there is a skilful ruse. The average man in the street, or the average woman in the home needs to be shown the ruse. The profound caddishness that sent Fisher and More to the block on Tower Hill would never have suggested itself to the average Tower Hill folk who crowded round these two Englishmen on their way to death. But the "cads"[10]—we can give them no other name—who had then the stranglehold on English liberty were determined to make England's two champions of liberty yield or die.

Yet the attainder for misprision of treason whilst committing Fisher and More to life-imprisonment had somewhat overreached itself. Whilst they were in the Tower, and not at liberty, their very imprisonment was a daily trumpet-call summoning Englishmen to defend the old liberties against the new tyranny. But the King and his Machiavellian minister were too far-seeing not to realize the silent strength that went out to the furthest parts of England from the prisoners in the Bell and Beauchamp Towers.

---

[10] A *cad* is an antiquated term for a man who behaves dishonourably, usually toward a woman. -Editor.

Yet seven months' confinement in the Tower made no change in the minds of the two prisoners; even though everything had been done that could well be done to bend their spirit. If the sentence of life-imprisonment could be changed into a sentence of death by a charge of treason perhaps the two men's courage could be broken down.

Accordingly in the November of 1534, the Tudor device called Parliament passed a Bill making it treason to deny the King's Supremacy or to affirm the Supremacy of the Pope. As a totalitarian contrivance it was perfect. By it Henry VIII justified the epigram of one of England's modern historians, Bishop Stubbs, who says that "from the beginning Henry wished to be king, the whole king and nothing but the king; and in the end he wished to be in regard to the Church of England, the Pope, the whole Pope and something more than the Pope."

But a prisoner in the Tower like Fisher makes no denials or affirmations. The law looks on him as dead. It was therefore necessary to entrap Fisher into some definite denial of Royal Supremacy or affirmation of Papal Supremacy—even by the worse than lie of a royal "confidence-trick." Hence the Machiavellian invitation to write his mind through the King's minister, Cromwell, to the King, that a charge of treason might be brought against him.

4. Notice the old scholar's laconic and adroit "hip-throw" of his opponents. Not only does he profess his willingness to swear to the lawful

succession of Elizabeth; he even gives the constitutional reason of his willingness. But the rest he passes over with the laconic ambiguity: "Albeit I refused to swear to some other parcels because that my conscience would not serve me so to do."

The present writer can never read these words of the old, courteous, unbeaten Yorkshireman without crying out: "Well played! England at its best is answering by your mouth."

The saint comes as near as a saint can come to explicit contempt in his next pathetic plea about "his shirt, his suit (which he spells s-u-t-e) and his other clothes . . . that be ragged and rent to shamefully."

He passes from the business of the oath as abruptly as if to say: "That's that! You know my mind without asking me. Give up your stage-playing and come to realities—my shirt, my suit, my clothes are in shameful rags—I am ill-fed I am shivering with London winter-fog. I beseech you to be good, master, unto me in my necessity."

Then the "good Master Cromwell" prepared to answer this question of the shamefully ragged shirt and suit and clothes—with the axe!

5. Read once again, with or without tears, this moan of a breaking heart: "And, as our Lord knoweth, I have nothing left unto me for to provide me better, but as my brother of his own purse layeth out for me to his own hindrance."

From what we know of our hero, master Cromwell would never have heard of his prisoner's ragged shirt and suit and clothes—of his slender fare—and his cold body—had there been no Robert Fisher, who tried to help his bishop-brother, even "to his own great hindrance."

If ever a great drama of Fisher has its Shakespeare, this Robert Fisher will have no mean or simple part. When our saint went to Rochester as its bishop, Robert went with him as joint-partner in the great business of administering the poorest diocese of England for the glory of God, and the furtherance of God's poor. The two brothers were one when charity called.

But the King's business which had set brother against brother in many an English home or cloister and had parted More from his dear daughter Meg seems to have touched the unity between John and Robert Fisher. The Record Office contains a precious document giving the official record of the examination in the Tower of Richard Wilson, Fisher's servant, of George Golde, servant of Sir Edmund Walsingham, Lieutenant of the Tower, of John a Wood, servant of More, and others. The first answer of Wilson is that "About Midsummer (1534), he heard his master say to Mr. Walbere, Mr. Johnson, commissary of Rochester, and Mr. Robert Fisher, his brother, when they have persuaded him to take the Oath of Succession that he wished himself great misfortune if he went to any place for that purpose.'" In this scene Robert is playing Meg

More's part of allowing love of kindred to plead against a day-clear conscience.

Robert's brotherly love did not express itself in vain efforts to win this conscience from its supremacy in the Bishop's soul. This letter to Master Secretary witnesses to Robert's untiring and unselfish effort to give the prisoner some of the necessaries of food and clothing.

His last service to his prisoner-brother was about Candlemas. He came, no doubt with food, and told his brother about the Act of Supremacy; whereupon the Bishop "toke up his hands and blessed him, saying, 'Is it so?' He went on to tell him of something never heard before, that words should be high treason and that in the Lower House there never was such a sticking at the passing of an Act; and at last (perhaps in prophetic self-defence), had added the word maliciously which was not worth . . ." Perhaps it was the last act of this faithful brother. We are told that in the spring of 1535 he died; and with his death a touch of winter entered the lonely cell in the Bell Tower. God rest his soul!

A slender anecdote coming to us as an answer of Richard Wilson is as fragrant as any spring wallflower on the Tower walls. "What have I sent to Mr. Moor or his servant?—Never sent anything concerning the King's matter either in word or writing. Sent to Mr. Moor's servant half a custard on Sunday last; and long since green sauce. More or his servant sent him an image of St. John and apples and oranges after the snow fell in winter.

"On New year's day sent him a paper with writing: £2,000 in gold and an image of the Epiphany."

Half a custard—I expect the larger half—and green sauce from the practical Yorkshireman. A jest of gold at the three Kings from the witty Londoner.

Non eripit mortalia
Qui regna dat celestia.

Grace does not destroy nature; but leaves the two men the same men to the end.

There is one incident recorded in the depositions of Wilson that we are unable to classify as tragedy or comedy. Perhaps it is both. Be it remembered that Wilson is Fisher's servant; and George [Golde] is servant to the Lieutenant of the Tower. George could be, naturally, a very valuable friend or a very dangerous spy. What evidence we have seems to honour him as the martyr's friend. But he had his limitations. He was not always as reliable as he was willing; for reasons made plain in the following: "Afterwards I heard him say to George that he saw no great peril in the Statute unless it were done or spoken maliciously. The next night Fisher wrote a letter to More, which was not sealed or closed, and told him, if George were sober to give it to him to be delivered; which he did."—Happily for the Bishop it was one of George's good days.

6. The Bishop's meek request that "I may borrow some books to stir my devotion more effectually these holy days for the comfort of my soul." What torment for the old book-lover whose library at Rochester was the talk of European scholars and was the only riches of his poor house.

In default of books to read the lonely prisoner set about books to write. In the fourteen months of his imprisonment he found time to write two treatises in English and one in Latin.

The two English books are addressed to his half-sister Catherine, a nun in the Dominican Convent at Dartford. The first is called *A Spiritual Consolation*—a subject dear to the hearts of the two lonely prisoners; who both gave us treatises on the subject. But in each book the writer is revealed in every line he writes. Though both succeed in hiding from their readers that the writer is in prison, awaiting death, Fisher's *Consolation* is largely compounded of a wholesome dread of eternal woe. But More's Dialogue on Comfort contrives to turn all human mishap and even eternal punishment almost into a jest! Fisher's grave book raises your heart to heaven. But More's book raises many a laugh to his reader's lips.

Fisher's *Way of Perfect Religion* is, perhaps designedly, the resolution of the minor chord of its predecessor. It is altogether in the atmosphere of divine love.

His Latin work on prayer might almost be looked on as a summary of what St. Thomas Aquinas has written in his *Summa Theologica*. This work of Fisher's awaits its translator and publisher—for once translated and published it will not long await its readers.

7. Fisher's request "for some priest within the Tower to hear my confession against this holy time" of Christmas may sound unintelligible to modern Protestants in these days when every prison counts a chaplain amongst its paid officials. But the ages of faith present us with not a few problems of which this is one. Leaving to other hands the historical discussion of the matter we may quote the words of Fisher's best modern biographer, Fr. Bridgett: "Whether Fisher was allowed to receive Communion then, or at Easter, or before his death we cannot now discover."

In this way the saint was asked to share the loneliness of heart that cried out: "My God, my God, why hast Thou forsaken me?"

Here ends what Fisher's letter to Cromwell called upon us to say; and what we have said so ill.

XXI - Job's Comfortors - The Hierarchy that Failed

Everything we know of Fisher tells us of a conscience that was sensitive even to the verge of scrupulosity. Such a sensitiveness when in isolation tends to be morbid if it is not controlled by a resolute will. When Fisher found himself in the Bell Tower, alone not merely in body but in mind, some strength other than human must have steeled him in his convictions. His isolation was not merely that of a churchman from a layman; but of a bishop from his fellow-bishops.

Had these bishops been notoriously unspiritual or unlearned, his lonely furrow would have seemed less self-assertive. But unspirituality and ignorance cannot be fastened on Fisher's fellow-bishops except by a historic assumption against the facts.

There is some evidence, though not convincing, that the day after Fisher's imprisonment the Oath of Succession (and Supremacy) was again tendered to him; and again refused. Cromwell may have been so ignorant of Fisher's strength of will as to think that a taste of the Tower—and a sight of the axe!—might cow him into submission. But though Fisher's trust in his own strength was always of the weakest his daily prayer was petitioning and meriting another strength which brought him daily perseverance.

When the commissioners who seized the goods of the Bishop made their inventory, they noted in the little study: "divers glasses and boxes with syrups, sugars, stilled water, and other certain trash, sent to my lord." If these are evidence of a delicate constitution, somewhat self-conscious and self-defensive, confinement in the Tower must have been a refinement of mental torture.

This torture was only heightened by the Job's comforters whom the royal largesse allowed or commanded to visit him. Laymen whom the King trusted by reason of their servile capacity came to prove how foolish it was to be alone in withstanding a king whose favour might mean a cardinal's hat and whose disfavours might mean death. Their visits were lost time. To use one of the martyr's laconic phrases "they went even as they came."

A harder trial to the English and Catholic blood in his veins was when his King sent visitors who were brother bishops. The old manuscript life dares to give the names, not of all, but of three, perhaps because it can also give an account of their bitter repentance.

The three names are, Bishop Stokesley of London, Bishop Gardiner of Winchester, Bishop Tunstal of Durham. Had Fisher been willing (as More wittily said) "to pin his faith on any man's back," no men in England would have equalled these three in their hopes of changing Fisher's faith. No bishops or theologians could have offered Fisher such arguments for accepting a Royal Supremacy which the Pope himself with Rome's habitual knowledge of the facts had not condemned.

It is to the credit of these three Job's comforters that they unplayed their part in after years by a repentance which was often bitter self-reproach. But no doubt if their pleading with the martyr for the King was ineffectual the martyr's pleadings to God for them was not unheard.

At another time the King (i.e., Cromwell, who was now and for a few years the King's political alter ego and deputy conscience) sent some six or seven bishops to do what the three most learned bishops could not do. They succeeded no better than their predecessors. If the old manuscript writer is to be trusted, the group of bishops had to listen to some plain-speaking from the old prisoner on the brink of the grave. He could hardly help reminding these shepherds that, whilst wolves were ravening the flock, shepherds should not be making compromises with the wolf. Great as were the evils besetting Holy Mother Church he foresaw still worse, because (to use a striking phrase of the chronicler) "the forte is betrayed even of those that should have defended it." Then the six or seven defenders of the fort went out leaving imprisoned within London's great fort a soul, "free with the freedom wherewith Christ had made him free."

In 1529, when More, lately made Lord Chancellor, opened the famous Long Parliament[11] in the great hall at Blackfriars, even his rare insight could hardly have foreseen that one of its most famous Acts would be his indictment for misprision of treason.

After prorogation it met again in the November of 1534. It was still a Parliament of King's men; but of King's men whom the late royal doings had made a little apprehensive of the King's will. One of the chief points of the King's will was to make certain the attainder of Fisher and More for misprision of treason. Legal experts are agreed that the imprisonment of the two Englishmen was illegal because it was not covered by the Act of Succession. To give an air of decent legality to the King's injustice, Parliament had to pass a second Act of Attainder against the two prisoners in the Tower.

But the most famous—or infamous—doing of this Long Parliament was the passing of the Act of (Royal) Supremacy. Viewed historically it was an Act without precedent in the annals of England and indeed of the Christian world. By making the King the sole legislative, judicial and executive head and governor in the realm it achieved the Totalitarian State with an effectiveness which still serves as a

---

[11] The "Long Parliament," is a name also given to the Parliament of 1641-1660. This "Long Parliament" today is called the "Reformation Parliament." -Editor's note.

model for statesmen of the same bewildered way of thinking.

Although the Act was passed in November, it was not to become operative till February 1st, 1535. Cromwell needed time to elaborate with his genius for elaborating, his programme of action. In the event his plans proved so well thought out that they worked without a hitch.

In the Letters and Papers (1535) edited by James Gairdner there is an unforgettable entry 190:

1. Renunciation by Thos. (Cranmer) Abp. of Canterbury of the jurisdiction of the see of Rome, and of all allegiance to any foreign potentate.

10 Feb.

2. Stephen (Gardiner), Bp. of Winchester. 10 Feb.
3. John (Clerk), Bp. of Bath and Wells.   10 Feb.
4. John (Stokesley), Bp. of London.   11 Feb.
5. Thomas (Goodrich), Bp. of Ely.   11 Feb.
6. John (Longland), Bp. of Lincoln. 1   3 Feb.
7. John (Kyte), Bp. of Carlisle.   15 Feb.
8. Edward (Lee), Abp. of York.   26 Feb.
9. John (Salcott), Bp. of Bangor.   26 Feb.
10. Robert (Sherburn), Bp. of Chichester.   26 Feb.
11. Roland (Lee), Bp. of Coventry and Lichfield.

27 Feb.

12. Cuthbert (Tunstall), Bp. of Durham.   2 Mar.
13. Richard (Nix), Bp. of Norwich.   7 Mar.
14. Charles (Booth), Bp. of Hereford.   18 Mar.
15. Richard (Rawlins), Bp. of St. Davids.   4 Apl.

Only two diocesan Bishops did not make this declaration and take the Oath of Royal Supremacy —our martyr, John (Fisher), Bp. of Rochester, and George (Athequa), O.P., Bp. of Llandaff, the Spanish confessor of Queen Catherine.

On February 2nd, Robert Fisher came to the Tower and told the Bishop of "the ACT OF SUPREME HEAD . . . when he take up his hands and blessed him saying: 'Is it so.'" It was the beginning of the end; and the Bishop's words mean that he knew it to be so.

As, later on, printed copies of the Act were to be had, it seems likely that on February 1st, these copies were available at the London booksellers. Printed proclamations would be seen in many public places. Robert Fisher seems to have at once given accurate information to his brother in the Bell Tower.

XXII - The Monk's Books - Mr. Moore was Merry -The Martyr Sleeps

Dear reader, at the beginning of this book on a martyr I warned you not to expect any glorious miracle or saying or action, such as you find in the primitive "Acts of the Martyrs." In the Acts of St. John Fisher, Bishop and Martyr, all is the sober prose or plain-song of martyrdom.

For this reason, in lieu of the miracles which are lacking I will now offer your intelligence and faith and love, the sober prose of a list of happenings in the last days of our martyr. It will be for you to realize, as you read, the truth of the old proverb "*Sunt lacrymae rerum.*"

> 1535 May 4. Martyrdom of Hale, Reynolds
> and Carthusians.
> „ 7.   Fisher before Council.
> „ 13.   (?)
> „ 20.   Made Cardinal
> June 3. Questioned in the Tower
> 12, 14.   „ „ „ „ „
> 17.   Trial at WESTMINSTER.
> 19.   Martyrdom of three Carthusians.
> June 22. (Monday) St. Alban's Day. FISHER
> BEHEADED ON TOWER HILL

The martyrdom of Hale, Reynolds, and the Carthusians on May 4th was calculated, if not designed, to cow all opposition to the will of the new Supreme Head of the Church of England.

On June 8th, when Wilson, Fisher's servant, was examined in the Tower he gave us a precious record which shall be set down as it stands in the Record Office: "Between the examinations (i.e., May 7-13) George (servant of the Lieutenant of the Tower) brought Fisher certain scrolls of paper with lead in some others with an agg [let or] dry point so that

105

they could not be well read; which George said his master had bade him cut out of the monks' books.

"In one was written: '*Pasce oves meos*,' etc., 'and I am sure that these words Christ spake Himself, and dare take that quarrel to my death.'

"In another place he read: My Lord ye should not judge me to death this day; for if ye should first condemn yourself and all your predecessors which were no simple sheep in this flock but great bell wethers. And my Lord if ye would in detestation of this opinion dig up the bones of all our predecessors and burn them yet should not that turn me from this Faith.'

"Could not read any more. Showed them to his master; who said: 'They be gone. God have mercy on their souls!'" "And when they were alive, Fisher said, referring to the said monks under examination: 'I pray God that no vanity subvert them.'"

Fisher's two remarks are not indifference. They are the studied self-control, under fire, of the commanding officer!

On Friday (after Ascension Thursday), May 7th, Cromwell and his men came to question Fisher that he might be cowed into submission or trapped into treasonable answer that would mean death. The questioning took place in Fisher's room in the Bell Tower. The faithful Wilson hid himself "outside the partition," a self-appointed ear-witness. Here he overheard the short passage at arms between his master and Bedyll, Clerk of the Council, Archdeacon of Cornwall. Bedyll's argument for the King's Supremacy was so bad that Wilson told his master after supper how even he could see its weakness."

Then *"the Bishop asked if he thought he had been too quick with Mr. Bedyll; and respondent said: No."*

(N.B.—There are no miracles in Fisher's life—and after death, not enough for the ordinary process of canonization. But to the present unworthy writer, this question put by the Cardinal to his servant is worth many a miracle. It is the transcendent miracle of a perfect grace-begotten but wholly human act.)

The group of questioners earned nothing by their visit. But after they had gone More sent to him a copy of the letter he had written to Margaret Roper, giving a minute account of his sayings and his silence before the Council. Again he wrote to More concerning the word maliciously in the Act of Supremacy. More thought that their answers would be much alike and that the Council would suspect that one had "taken light" of the other; and warned Fisher to avoid all suspicion.

The exchange of letters had assured each one that they were both agreed not to take the Oath of Supremacy. This assurance was the more necessary because it seems that each martyr was told as a certainty that the other had taken the Oath.

In referring to this, George, on one of his best days, stumbled upon a statement of the matter which has no equal as a cameo of the two martyrs: ". . . heard him say that Mr. More was merry and my Lord was satisfied!"

Of the second examination by the Council, Fisher said laconically, "the Council was gone even as it came."

About this time an event occurred which had an effect on Fisher's life and death beyond all reckoning. On May 10th, Paul III created seven Cardinals, among whom was Fisher, who was made Cardinal-priest of the title of St. Vitalis. The Pope's motive in making Fisher a cardinal has been variously interpreted. It must remain for ever hidden in the realm of motives and intentions. If Henry's agent at the Papal Court, Sir Gregory Casale, is to be believed, his letter from Rome on May 29th would assure us that he had had an interview with the Pope. His Holiness was surprised to think that his honouring Fisher would create trouble at the English Court, as in making Fisher a cardinal he had wished to give pleasure to Henry!

This throws light on the fact that on the Saturday after the second examination the said George Golde said to Fisher that he was to be made a cardinal. Then, said Fisher, "Cardinal! Then I perceive it was not for nought that my Lord Chancellor did ask me when I heard from my master the Pope, and said that *there was never man that had exalted the Pope as I had*." (These words must never be forgotten on the martyr's feast.) But in

answer to George's news the Cardinal said with
unusual vehemence "... that he set as much by that
as by a rush under his feet." His own version of this
is that in the presence of Golde and Wilson he said
that "if the Cardinal's hat were laid at his feet, he
would not stoop to take it up, he did set so little by
it."

To Henry must be allowed the grimmest repartee
of his century. On being told that the Pope had
made Fisher a cardinal he said angrily: "Let the
Pope send him a hat when he will. But I will so
provide that whensoever it cometh he shall wear it
on his shoulders—for head he shall have none to set
it on." Some historians, on what principle does not
appear, have denied this repartee. But it is not
unreasonable to argue that the man who was
capable of the greater was capable of the less; and it
is surely a greater inhumanity to behead an
innocent victim than to talk or even rage about it.

On Thursday, June 17th, the great gateway of the
Tower opened to a company of men-at-arms "with
halberts, bills and other weapons." The Tower axe,
edge forward, was borne before an old tottering
prisoner who seemed too ill even to walk. The
prisoner was John Fisher, Cardinal Bishop of
Rochester, who was that day to go through the
tragedy of a mock trial of high treason for being of
the same faith as all his fellow-Englishfolk had been
for a thousand years.

The grim picturesque procession moved slowly at the old man's pace, to the Tower jetty where boats awaited them, for a short row to the jetty close to Westminster Hall. If Fisher did not go from the Tower to Westminster on foot but by boat, it was not through kindness or courtesy to his office or rank but through fear that his age and illness might give them a corpse to bury rather than a prisoner to condemn.

There was a fitness in his coming to trial in Westminster Hall. It had been built by William Rufus, who might have forestalled the totalitarianism of Henry had not the cowed episcopate been led by an Anselm.

Moreover, the great Minster in whose liberties Fisher met trial was dedicated to St. Peter; English devotion to St. Peter had built the Minster; and English devotion to St. Peter was being put to the test by the trial of John Fisher.

The Hall of Rufus was still murmurous of the Carthusians, the Bridgettines and the secular priests who had been tried and pronounced guilty of the charge now brought against Fisher. Their glorious constancy even through the horrors of hanging and disembowelling would have encouraged Fisher, if that blessed martyr even in the high art of martyrdom had not always heard the Master's words that "it is a more blessed thing to give than to receive."

Only a legal interest attaches to the fact that the judicial murder of an illustrious and loyal Englishman was technically a trial before the King's Bench. When we know that it was presided over by Audley, Lord Chancellor, and that it included Mr. Secretary Cromwell and the Earl of Wiltshire (Ann Boleyn's father), its gesture towards legal impartiality deceived no one—not even the King's men.

Something more than a legal interest—perhaps even a pathological interest—attaches to the following entries in Cromwell's note-book at this time. The notes are headed by Cromwell "Remembrances at my next going to the Court. . . To send letters and money into Ireland, and advise the Deputy of the King's pleasure.

"To advertise the King of the ordering of Master Fisher and to show him the indenture which I have delivered to the Solicitor. To know his pleasure touching Master More. . . . WHEN MASTER FISHER SHALL GO TO EXECUTION and also the other. What shall be done further concerning Master More. The conclusion for my Lord of Suffolk. TO SEND TO THE KING BY RAFFE THE BEHAVIOUR OF MASTER FISHER."

We have expressed our wonder whether the interest of this leaf of Remembrances is not chiefly pathological. The intelligence which could organize into a political or administrative unity so many different functions, yet could arrange the death of illustrious citizens with the detachment of a cargo-checker is a problem in psychology which offers as alternatives either mental or moral deficiency of an unusual type.

Master. . . . Master. . . . Master Fisher. Never once Cardinal or even Bishop Fisher at the indictment! Part of the proof that Fisher by his heroic virtue might have been canonized as a confessor if not as a martyr, is the Saint's unfailing patience and courtesy with this unscrupulous cad who could not be as courteous as a charge-sheet. But as he, too, was one of Henry's victims, may God rest his soul.

As the manuscript contemporary life of Fisher is now in the hands of the public, the detailed account of the trial, which must be substantially accurate, may be taken as read. All we need know in our love of the martyr is the fact that like all his fellow-martyrs in Henry's reign, he died because he would not affirm on oath the Supremacy of the Sovereign and deny on oath the Supremacy of the Pope.

For the third time within a few weeks the liberties of St. Peter's, Westminster, were witness of a peerless group of loyal Englishmen condemned to death for being loyal Catholics. To us who are witnesses of the slowness and thoroughness of a modern capital trial it seems incredible that the trial of the most illustrious Bishop of the realm should be completed in a few hours.

A trivial incident may or may not cast light on the length of Fisher's trial. It was by river that the old dying Bishop went from Tower jetty to

Westminster. But he came back on horseback, not by boat. It may be that on the way thither the swift current of the Thames was sweeping in—and that it had not yet turned when the trial was over. Or it may be that, by the King's pleasure, the citizens of London were to witness what it meant to cross the King's will.

Be that as it may, when the trial was over, the procession of men-at-arms with halberts and bills and other weapons was reformed—but the axe—still borne aloft, had its cutting-edge towards the condemned prisoner!

Dear reader! be not disappointed if our hero, again copying his Master, flies into the silences, himself alone. The four days he spent in immediate preparation for certain death have left us no authentic last words, no touching farewells, no dying messages. The old Yorkshireman has something to do on a day to come—how near or how far he knows not—and he is preparing for this unknown by quietly doing the business of to-day.

His nameless biographer has a phrase which we must cull if only for its perfection of quality: "Although he looked daily for death, yet could ye not have perceived him one whit dismayed or disquieted thereat neither in word nor countenance, but still continued his trade of constancy and patience."

Yet out of the silences of the Bell Tower there come two carillons of the Saint's "trade of constancy and patience." The first is almost the Saint's only claim to humour; the second would base the only charge of sloth.

This is the first: One of these four days the cook (or was it the faithful Robert?) brought him no dinner. Next day when the cook came, the Saint asked him why he had not brought him his dinner:

"Sir," said the cook, " it was commonly talked all the town over that you should have died that day, and therefore I thought it but in vain to dress anything for you."

"Well," said he merrily to him again, "for all that report, thou seest me yet alive. And therefore whatsoever news thou shalt have of me, hereafter, let me no more lack my dinner; but make it ready as thou art wont to do. And if thou see me dead when thou comest, then eat it thyself. But I promise thee if I be alive: I mind by God's grace to eat never a bit the less."

That is in its essence Merry England—soon to be slain as a traitor on Tower Hill.

This is the second and last carillon from the Bell Tower. The listener-in would do well to hear it whilst on his knees. Moreover, in order to catch all its wealth of undertones and overtones he would do well to quiet and even forget merely human melodies lest they rend into discord this perfect *Introibo* of a martyr's morning sacrifice.

"After the Lieutenant received this bloody writ (for Fisher's execution on the morrow) . . . in the morning before five of the clock he came to him in the Bell Tower, finding him yet asleep in his bed and waked him . . . and told him at the last that he was come to signify unto him that the King's pleasure was he should suffer death that forenoon.

" 'Well,' quoth this blissful father, 'if this be your errand you bring me no great news, for I have long time looked for this message. And I must humbly thank the King's Majesty that it pleaseth him to rid me from all this worldly business. And I thank you also for your tidings.

"But I pray you, Master Lieutenant, when is my hour that I must go hence?'

"'Your hour,' said the Lieutenant, must be nine of the clock.'

"'And what hour is it now?' said he.

"'It is now about five,' said the Lieutenant.

'Well then,' said he, 'let me by your patience sleep an hour or two. For I have slept very little this night. And yet to tell the truth, not for any fear of death, I thank God, but by reason of my great infirmity and weakness.' . . . the Lieutenant departed from him. And so the prisoner falling again to rest slept soundly two hours and more."

Dear reader! had you and I been in that room on that June morning whilst our hero, our martyr, our saint, was sleeping, we should have been on our knees weeping—yet not sobbing lest any unchecked sob of ours might wake him before his Angel awoke him to his last few steps towards eternal life.

When he awoke he prepared for death, to use his own phrase, as if for a wedding. He laid aside his hair-shirt!—the self-imposed penance of a prisoner for whose love of the Crucified even prison-penance was not enough.

He bade his man lay out a clean white shirt—and his best clothes—well brushed as might be.

He had overslept a little, so that when Master Lieutenant came at nine he was not quite ready. He asked his man to fetch his fur tippet and put it about his neck. The old commanding officer was afraid not of being afraid but, through weakness, of seeming afraid in the face of death.

Before leaving for the last time his room in the Bell Tower he took up a little book of the New Testament—made the sign of the Cross—and feebly went down the stairs.

He was seen to be so weak that two of the Tower-men had to carry him the few yards to the gate where they awaited to deliver their prisoner to the Sheriff of London for beheading. Whilst waiting for the formality of being handed over to the Sheriff he rose from the carrying-chair. His weakness made him lean against the wall. Then opening the little book of the New Testament he prayed God to send him some word of strength.

Opening the book he read from the Gospel of St. John, the words his Redeemer spoke to His Father in the Supper room. "This is eternal life to know

Thee, the only true God and Him whom Thou hast sent, Jesus Christ.

"I have glorified Thee on earth. I have finished the work Thou gayest me to do.

"And now glorify Thou me, Father, with Thyself, with the glory which I had," etc.

Then he shut the book, saying "Here is even learning enough for me even to my life's end." The old Catholic humanist and lover of learning was "satisfied."

A great mustering of the Sheriff's men, with weapons, guarded him the remaining few yards from the Tower Gate to Tower Hill. As before, he was carried almost helpless because of his infirmities. Yet when he reached the steps that led to the scaffold he courteously refused help and almost ran up, as if with unseen help.

The morning sun, now in the south-east, "shone very bright in his face, whereupon he said: 'Draw nigh to Him and be enlightened. And your countenances shall not be confounded.'

"The headsman begged his forgiveness. 'I forgive thee,' he said, 'with all my heart. And I trust thou shalt see me overcome this storm lustily.'

"Then was he stripped and he stood in his doublet and hose—by his leanness a very Image of Death." The crowds that were around the scaffold marvelled at the cruelty that could bring such a man—such an Englishman—to the block.

On the scaffold he obeyed the "King's pleasure," by speaking but a few words. He said he was about to die for the faith—that hitherto by God's grace he had not feared—but that he asked their prayers lest at the very stroke of death he might not stand steadfast. His last words were a prayer to God to save the King and the Realm.

The old orator of the English Episcopate could still be recognized in the clear, far-carrying voice that for the last time reached to the ends of an English crowd. And truly did it reach not only to the ends of the Tower Hill crowd, but to the ends of his beloved birth-land, and to the ends of the earth: for it broadcast from the Hill of royal hate the prayer of a very courteous gentleman, an undaunted defender of liberty, a hero, a saint.

The headsman bound a kerchief about his eyes—those honest, far-seeing eyes, that: "were long and round, neither full black nor full grey." All the while they were readying him for death he was praying as the priest prays whilst readying himself for morning Mass.

He bowed his knees. Then like his Master in the Olive Garden he stretched his withered body on the scaffold—his neck resting on the block.

The headsman struck one blow at the outstretched body and the head of the first canonized Cardinal Martyr, like the Baptist's head he had so long honoured, had won its title to a place for ever on the Altar of Sacrifice !

118

XXIII -Ira Regis Mors Est

All day long a great company of men-at-arms with halberts and weapons guarded a naked body on a scaffold at Tower Hill.

At nightfall, when the Bride of Christ is remembering how her Bridegroom was laid in His tomb, two of the soldiers took the martyr's body upon their halberts to the graveyard of All Hallows Church, hard by. There on the north side of the churchyard close to the wall, they rested the body till their halberts had dug a grave." And therein without any reverence they tumbled the body of this holy prelate and blessed martyr all naked and flat upon his belly, without either sheet or other accustomed things belonging to a Christian man's burial."

The blissful martyr's head, first parboiled in water, was set on high on London Bridge among the two glorious companies of Englishmen who had outrun him in the race for martyrdom.

Then there happened the sole reputed miracle in this wondrous life. The martyr's head, though exposed to the summer sun, was seen not to dry nor shrink. Daily, men said, his cheeks " grew beautiful with a comely red, so that in his life-time he never looked so well. The crowds that came to look upon the martyr's head said he was looking upon them and silently speaking to them. At last these crowds became so great that no cart nor even horse could pass. Then came the 'King's pleasure' that the head should be taken down and cast away, and its place given to the head of his fellow-martyr, More."

No sooner had the Pope heard that one of his cardinals had laid down his life in defence of Papal Authority than he began the long-lasting work of fitly honouring a martyr.

A special Consistory was summoned to hear the account of how, by an unheard-of crime, a cardinal had been put to death for keeping his loyalty to his lawful head.

In letters to Ferdinand, King of the Romans, and to Francis, King of France, he compared the martyr of Tower Hill with the "blissful martyr of Canterbury—adding the significant words that whereas Henry II "slew the defender of the rights of one particular Church, this man (Henry VIII has slain) is the defender of the rights of the Church Universal!"

Such public and unwonted praise by a Pope was almost the equivalent of canonization. Yet Rome's concern for peace delayed the official canonization until four centuries of misunderstanding had led the severed parts of England to feel the need of reunion through mutual understanding.

It has remained for Pope Pius XI to finish what Paul III begun. Few acts of His Holiness have surpassed in pontifical insight his canonization of St. John Fisher, Cardinal-Priest of Saint Vitalis, and St. Thomas More, once Lord Chancellor of England.

These two leaders of the clergy and laity of Mary's Dowry have been given the full ecumenical publicity of canonization not merely as defenders of that divine institution the Papacy, but of that earlier divine institution, human liberty. For both institutions the two died, as they had lived after their own manner, for:

". . . even on the morn they died MR. MORE WAS MERRY AND MY LORD SATISFIED."

Made in the USA
Middletown, DE
17 August 2020

15227606R00076